WHEN THE NEWS
WENT LIVE

Standing alone (left) at Main and Akard, Bob Huffaker broadcasts as the motorcade passes, his mobile unit engulfed by the crowd. *Photograph courtesy The Sixth Floor Museum at Dealey Plaza. Tom Dillard Collection*, Dallas Morning News

WHEN THE NEWS WENT LIVE

DALLAS 1963

50TH ANNIVERSARY EDITION

BOB HUFFAKER, BILL MERCER,
GEORGE PHENIX, WES WISE

Foreword by Dan Rather

TAYLOR TRADE PUBLISHING
Lanham New York Boulder Toronto Plymouth, UK

973.922
Huffaker

Published by Taylor Trade Publishing
An imprint of The Rowman & Littlefield Publishing Group, Inc.
4501 Forbes Boulevard, Suite 200, Lanham, Maryland 20706
www.rowman.com

10 Thornbury Road, Plymouth PL6 7PP, United Kingdom

Distributed by National Book Network

British Library Cataloguing in Publication Information Available

Library of Congress Cataloging-in-Publication Data

Huffaker, Robert, 1936–
   When the news went live : Dallas 1963 / Bob Huffaker, Bill Mercer, George Phenix, Wes Wise. — 50th anniversary edition.
      pages cm
   Includes index.
   ISBN 978-1-58979-895-3 (cloth : alk. paper) — ISBN 978-1-58979-896-0 (electronic) 1. Kennedy, John F. (John Fitzgerald), 1917–1963—Assassination. 2. Television journalists—Texas—Dallas—Biography. 3. Dallas (Tex.)—Biography. 4. Television broadcasting of news—Social aspects—United States. I. Mercer, Bill, 1926– II. Phenix, George. III. Wise, Wes. IV. Title.
   E842.9.W448 2013
   973.922092—dc23
                                            2013013991

♾™ The paper used in this publication meets the minimum requirements of American National Standard for Information Sciences—Permanence of Paper for Printed Library Materials, ANSI/NISO Z39.48–1992.

Printed in the United States of America

CONTENTS

DEDICATION

To our KRLD colleagues and our fellow journalists who rose to the challenge of 1963. To my wife, Veva, and our sons, Kevin Huffaker and Zachary Vonler. To John F. Kennedy's memory. And to all who seek wisdom through lessons of history. **Bob Huffaker**

To my wife of sixty-six years, Ilene, who persevered through my rambunctious fifty years of broadcasting; our children, Laura, Evan, Martin and David, and our beautiful and intelligent granddaughters, Maile, Emma, Myra, Rachel, Sadie, Amaris, and Felicia; to the gallant journalists who preceded and taught us, the wonderful people we served with, and to the young journalists who follow: may you strive always to report the truth. And to our chief writer, researcher, editor and friend, Bob Huffaker, without whose talent and intelligence this would never have been written. **Bill Mercer**

To the reporters of today—from the journalists of yesterday. To my kids and grandkids, and to Lyn Ellen Lacy, my Mystery Woman.
George Phenix

To my wife, Sally, who was by my side at the Trade Mart when we got the awful news; to my son, Westley, Jr., who placed flowers at the grassy knoll; to my younger son and daughter, Wyn and Wendy, who gave of their time with their father to journalism. To the gallant citizens of Dallas, who suffered excruciating shock and pain, frustrating shame and unjustified blame, yet emerged with even greater character and compassion. **Wes Wise**

ACKNOWLEDGMENTS

We are grateful to the Sixth Floor Museum at Dealey Plaza for permissions to reprint images and quote from archived KRLD News tapes in their Bob Huffaker and other collections—and for their dedication to preserving the memory of President John F. Kennedy, the history of his tragic death, and the broader view of his life and U.S. history. These professionals are engaged in outreach to the world, and in particular to its young.

We thank our CBS News colleagues Dan Rather and Bob Schieffer, and PBS stalwart Jim Lehrer for their help and encouragement.

Daniel Irvin Rather, author of *Rather Outspoken* and managing editor of AXS TV's *Dan Rather Reports,* has been a friend and colleague since 1961, when he became CBS Southwest Bureau Chief and began his long and distinguished career with that network.

Bob Lloyd Schieffer, who moderates CBS's *Face the Nation* and lends sanity to Sunday mornings, is unusually qualified for that political hot seat, having covered all four of the major Washington national assignments: the White House, the Pentagon, the U.S. Department of State, and the United States Congress. He has served CBS News in myriad on-air assignments since his first anchor job at Fort Worth's WBAP-TV. Before moving to television, he was a reporter for the *Fort Worth Star-Telegram,* once hauling Marguerite Oswald to Dallas police headquarters after her son shot the president.

We are grateful to James Charles Lehrer, who, as City Editor of the old *Dallas Times Herald,* put up with Bob Huffaker and Frank Glieber invading his city room to broadcast KRLD radio newscasts daily over a prehistoric olive-drab microphone. Jim Lehrer went ahead to cut the trail for public television news, co-founding what is now the *PBS NewsHour* with his partner Robert MacNeil, and, from the days of his local public television *Newsroom*, providing a reliable and determinedly undramatic voice of news to the world for four decades. His fine book *Tension City* chronicles the history of U.S. televised presidential debates. This soft-spoken ex-Marine moderator deserves special credit for not decking either candidate during his twelfth nationally televised presidential debate: the Obama-Romney spectacle of October 3, 2012, in Denver.

We thank our sturdy floor director Benny Molina, who stayed cool, friendly, and professional through all of our broadcasts, especially those from police headquarters in the uncertain hours and days after JFK's assassination.

We are grateful to writer and reporter Dean Angel and our Dutch film chief, Henk Dewit, who, during the frantic post-assassination days and nights, pushed the 16mm black-and-white through the big developers faster than normal limits just to get it on the air quicker—sometimes still a little damp and often streaked with developing soup. Gentle-spoken Dean and placidly fierce Henk were a good team. Dean had done his time in the U.S. Air Force, and Henk had done his in a Nazi work camp. Neither of them would have been distracted by the Devil himself.

We are glad that reporter Dick Wheeler joined KRLD News just in time to land in the midst of this peculiar historic story. He became news director of KRLD radio and then had the sense to sail away and live on his sailboat for some idyllic days.

We thank our departed KRLD colleagues: wise news director Eddie Barker; assistant news director Jim Underwood, a Marine veteran of Guadalcanal who ran *toward* the shots in Dealey Plaza; cool-headed cameramen Jim English and Gene Pasczalek; assignments editor Joe Dave Scott; Fort Worth correspondent Steve Pieringer; reporter and anchor Warren Fulks; versatile Frank Glieber; director Leigh Webb; film chief Henk Dewit; towering engineer Howard Chamberlain, Bill Mercer's bodyguard in the chaotic police headquarters; and engineer Otto Nilson, an old shipboard radio operator who knew the stars.

We are grateful to, and for, the talented Janet Harris and Veva Vonler, whose editorial wisdom guided this book, and Kay Banning for her detailed and scholarly index.

Among our competitors who covered this dark story, we are grateful to Bert Shipp, author of *Details at Ten*. Bert was WFAA-TV News, and plenty of fun.

We lift a cup to Hugh Aynesworth, the crew-cut *Dallas Morning News* aeronautics and space reporter who witnessed the president's murder in Dealey Plaza, sped to the Texas Theater and covered the arrest of Lee Oswald, then was with us in the police basement when Jack Ruby shot the young assassin to death. Hugh's book *JFK: Breaking the News* puts the facts in perspective.

To Kent Biffle, *Dallas Morning News* reporter and now author of *A Month of Sundays* and a great body of fine writing, who was among reporters held inside the Texas School Book Depository while police combed the place just after Oswald's hasty departure.

To Mike Cochran of the Associated Press, author of *Texas vs. Davis* and *Deliver Us from Evil*, who carried Oswald's coffin to the grave and is still a fine and prolific writer.

And to the late and beloved Alex Burton, author of *Just One Kiss, Baby*, for leaving his native Canada to soothe our tears with erudite and indomitable wit that was kind and well aimed.

Bob Huffaker, 2013

FOREWORD

There are times when it seems like yesterday. But more often it feels like an episode from another lifetime, and one feels fully the fifty years that separate us now from November 22, 1963.

Time does funny things to how we look back at history's landmarks, whether they are ones of triumph, like the first moon landing, or of tragedy, like the killing of a president. The millions of unfolding moments and perspectives that make up our understanding of an event in real time become condensed, distilled, and abbreviated into a handful of images and impressions. From the remove of passing decades we begin to imagine that we have gained a bird's-eye view of how things went. Seen from this vantage point, subtleties fade, and the confused and chaotic starts to appear orderly. The vagaries of chance seem in hindsight to become inexorable, fated.

So it has been with the assassination of President John Fitzgerald Kennedy and the dark days that followed. Today, mention of that time conjures the newsreel that has become our mental shorthand for all that happened in Dallas: the morning arrival at Love Field, Jackie's dress and pillbox hat, Abraham Zapruder's devastating footage of the fatal shot, the swearing in of President Lyndon Johnson aboard Air Force One, Jack Ruby's deadly lunge toward Lee Harvey Oswald. We see these things in our minds' eyes, and we tell ourselves that we have something approaching the full picture.

There are, famously and still, enough arguments, theories, and claims about the hows and whys of what happened in Dealey Plaza to fill a good-sized library. But the broader story, the story of a nation's descent into grief and shock over four unforgettable days, has hardened over the years into an apparently orderly and seamless narrative. Such is the view from afar.

For those who were in Dallas that day, though, the view was very different. The minutes, hours, and days after President Kennedy was shot provided no ready answers about just what was going on, what would happen next, or what any of it meant. There was, instead, a jumble of images, impressions, and information, very little of which had yet taken coherent form. Uncertainty reigned, not tidy story lines. For millions of Americans transfixed by the terrible breaking news, television emerged as a way to keep track of it all. But the journalists who brought the story to the television airwaves could only rely on their skill, their experience, and their stamina to make sense of what was clearly, at the time, the biggest story of their lives.

This book tells the stories of four men who were at the very epicenter of it all. Bob Huffaker, Bill Mercer, George Phenix, and Wes Wise were among those responsible for covering the assassination and its aftermath for KRLD, the Dallas CBS television and radio affiliate. From the presidential motorcade to Parkland Hospital, from Lee Harvey Oswald's shooting to the trial and lonesome death of Jack Ruby, they were there, on the inside. The view they were afforded of these events was unique; the tales they have to tell, one of a kind.

People often ask me "what it was really like" to be in Dallas on the day Kennedy was shot. It's a difficult question, one which I can only answer with my own, personal impressions. They are strong, and vivid, but they are necessarily and by definition limited. *When the News Went Live* provides an eloquent answer to that tough question, as four newsmen who were there, on the ground, tell how it "really was" through their eyes and ears.

Dan Rather, CBS News

PREFACE

Real News That Really Mattered

With three shots from a mail-order rifle, Lee Oswald set off a worldwide tragedy that developed too fast to print. Americans turned to their televisions and radios, and broadcasters assumed the task of reassuring a shocked nation and an anxious world. Broadcast journalism came of age in that crisis of grief and uncertainty, and as it drew its mourning audience, it helped to hold the nation together.

Radio and television reporters who were part of this watershed in broadcasting have had a half-century to consider events that were too fast and stunning to allow them detachment and reflection. Now with perspectives of age and history, three former colleagues join me in recording how we covered those terrible days. We describe what we remember and what we have learned, telling this story from four angles of vision and experience.

Weary of conspiracy theories, we concentrate upon describing these tragic events and telling how we reported them on the scene. This is our record of broadcast history, the story of how we reacted to this sudden and protracted national crisis when the news went live.

Television's cable news channels have all but overshadowed reporting from the three broadcast networks, and amid today's strident hypercoverage of celebrity murder and scandal, young people might find it strange that most reporters of the 1960s had little desire to sell the news. Except for that era's hotshot Top 40 radio, which screamed an overblown version of events akin to that of today's wilder cable channels, most broadcast journalists felt the duty to report only real news that really mattered. Finding and explaining it was our business.

The best broadcasters felt obligated to report with as much understanding as they could achieve and to speak with calm sense. Rather than letting audience ratings drive them to sensationalism, they strove to build audiences by being quick, accurate, and dependable. Radio had seen us through World War II, but in this 1963 crisis of sorrow, the central cohesive role fell to television for the first time. The friends who join me in telling this story were brought up in radio knowing that we were our communities' primary source of immediate information. We were keepers of a trust.

Bill Mercer, George Phenix, Wes Wise, and I were reporters for KRLD News, one of America's largest and best equipped news organizations. With both radio and television, we covered Texas and worked with Dan Rather, Walter Cronkite, and the rest of CBS News in bringing area news to the nation. When routine coverage of JFK's Dallas visit suddenly evolved into reporting a worldwide tragedy, we kept as calm as possible, to encourage the world to keep its sanity.

Bob Huffaker

THE WRITERS

Bob Huffaker, investigative reporter, broadcast the motorcade, then the scenes at Parkland Hospital and police headquarters, from where he narrated Oswald's murder on CBS. He interviewed the assassin's mother, and his courtroom interview with Jack Ruby won awards, as did his documentary on Black Muslims and other work. He has been an army officer, policeman, English professor, and editor for *Texas Monthly, Studies in the Novel,* and the *Modern Humanities Research Association Annual Bibliography.* Author of

Bob Huffaker

John Fowles, he has published in the *Dallas Observer, True West, Texas Parks and Wildlife,* and *Southern Humanities Review.* His defense of press freedom placed him in the Texas State University *Star* hall of fame.

Bill Mercer

Bill Mercer broadcast Oswald's midnight news conference, then the mourning in Dealey Plaza. Voice of the Dallas Cowboys, Texas Rangers, the University of North Texas, Southwest Conference, and Chicago White Sox, he was also an internationally popular wrestling announcer. Both the Texas Radio Hall of Fame and baseball's

All-Pro Hall of Fame honor him. He wrote a history of the LCI, a type of Navy combat landing craft on which he served in World War II. He is a professor of broadcast journalism at the University of North Texas.

George Phenix filmed Oswald's murder, the Parkland and Love Field scenes, and the Ruby trial. He also interviewed Warren Commission members in Dallas. Cofounder and publisher of *Texas Weekly,* for twenty years the state's top legislative newsletter, he has published several weekly newspapers and served as aide to Senator Lloyd Bentsen and Congressman Jake Pickle.

George Phenix

Wes Wise, whom Jack Ruby accosted on the day before shooting Oswald, was a witness in Ruby's trial. He filmed the attack on U. N. Ambassador Adlai Stevenson a month before the assassination. A pioneer of baseball play-by-play and writer for *Sports Illustrated, Time,* and *Life,* he was mayor of Dallas for five years and president of the Texas Municipal League. He won three Dallas Press Club "Katie" awards and Southern Methodist University's Southwest Journalism Forum Award. As mayor he guided Dallas through integration, helped save the Texas School Book Depository, and led the city in reclaiming its national reputation.

Wes Wise

MESSENGERS OF TRAGEDY

1

Covering a President Becomes a Nightmare

BOB HUFFAKER

I was lifting little children from the top of my mobile unit and handing them back to their parents. "I saw the president!" a little girl said as I took her under the arms and brought her down from the station wagon's luggage rack. Her father thanked me as he took her from my hands. In the canyon of towering buildings, the corner of Main and Akard was crowded with Dallasites who had cheered JFK as his motorcade passed. By the thousands they lined Main Street from Harwood to Houston Street. "He had a tan," a little boy observed as I set him down beside his mother. "Wasn't Jackie pretty?" she asked him as they melted into the throng.

I unslung the transistor radio from my shoulder and set it on the seat of the little black Mercury Comet—the odd unmarked wagon among our fleet of Pontiac Catalinas emblazoned with "KRLD News" in gold leaf beside the distinctive CBS eye. I replaced the two-way mike on its dashboard bracket and eased the station wagon through the dissolving crowd, most of them on their way to lunch after glimpsing John F. Kennedy and his radiant wife. With the car's low-band radio, I had broadcast a description of the motorcade passing through the jubilant crowd at the ticker-tape parade—the president golden bronze from his secret Addison's disease, Jackie in hot pink to her pillbox hat, and John and Nellie Connally waving from the jump seats ahead.

The transistor radio's earpiece enabled me to hear our big fifty-thousand-watt AM signal and take my cue in our live coverage of the president's visit. I had listened to my colleagues Frank Glieber and Wes Wise broadcasting from similar setups. Frank narrated Air Force One's

The two fated couples arrive at Dallas Love Field. *Photograph courtesy The Sixth Floor Museum at Dealey Plaza. Tom Dillard Collection,* Dallas Morning News

arrival at Love Field. Wes took over as the motorcade traveled Lemmon Avenue, then tossed it back for Frank's last broadcast from the airport.

As the motorcade neared the heart of Dallas, Frank introduced me on the air. I took his cue through my transistor's earpiece, and as soon as I heard the squelch break when he closed his mike switch, I began to describe the excited thousands lining Main Street behind police lines. Amid festoons of red, white and blue bunting, I described the scene as the parade passed in a whirl of ticker tape. After it had faded from sight, I talked about the president's political reasons for the Texas visit: to heal enmity between Lyndon Johnson's conservative wing of the Texas Democrats and the party's moribund populist faction led by the state's U.S. Senator Ralph Yarborough.

I stretched my broadcast toward the time when our news director, Eddie Barker, would take over from the huge new Trade Mart, where the president was to address a noon luncheon. JFK's Texas appearances were accomplishing their purpose, and his popularity was rising as he spoke in San Antonio and Houston the day before, then flew to Fort Worth for the night. We had begun the day's coverage with a live broadcast of the president's breakfast speech in Fort Worth. Now Eddie and our live TV cameras were ready to broadcast as JFK spoke to the crowd waiting at the Trade Mart.

In those days the venerable old metropolitan stations were still intact with clear-channel AM and FM radio along with the area's three network television stations and the three newspapers that owned them. The *Dallas Morning News* owned ABC affiliate WFAA-AM, FM, and TV Channel 8. The *Fort Worth Star-Telegram* held the NBC affiliate WBAP-AM, FM, and TV Channel 5. My paychecks came from the *Dallas Times-Herald*, which owned our CBS stations KRLD-AM, FM, and TV Channel 4. The television stations shared video with pool cameras at three locations: independent KTVT-TV Channel 11 fed the Fort Worth breakfast speech with help from Channel 5; Channel 8 fed the Love Field scene; and our Channel 4 cameras were ready at the Trade Mart.

As the motorcade faded from sight and the cheering crowd closed in to fill Main Street, I stayed on the air. I was reporting signs that Vice President Johnson and Governor John Connally had marked Yarborough for political extinction, splitting the state's Democrats and drawing JFK to mend Texas fences. I was glad to see the crowd's enthusiasm, and I was relieved to see no right-wing demonstrators like those who had jeered, spat upon, and struck U.N. Ambassador Adlai Stevenson with a placard the month before when he spoke in Dallas on United Nations Day.

While I went on broadcasting, a skinny young loner named Lee Oswald was killing John F. Kennedy barely more than a thousand yards away. I couldn't hear the three shots that echoed through Dealey Plaza—

The massive Main Street crowd surges forward to cheer JFK's motorcade.
Photograph courtesy The Sixth Floor Museum at Dealey Plaza. Photographer William Beal, Dallas Times Herald *Collection*

In the motorcade's wake, the throng closes in to fill Main Street. *Photograph courtesy The Sixth Floor Museum at Dealey Plaza. Photographer William Beal, Dallas Times Herald Collection*

named for the former *Dallas Morning News* publisher whose archconservative son was one of the president's bitter political enemies. Unlike his humanitarian father, Ted Dealey had turned the newspaper to the extreme right. When Kennedy had seen the paper's full-page attack ad against him that morning, he'd told Jackie, "We're headed into nut country today."

Mine was the last scheduled broadcast of the motorcade. Eddie Barker was up next, and I was glad to be off for the day. I'd been fueled with coffee and cigarettes since 4:30 that morning, and I was thinking about lunch as I drove the two blocks back to the station. When I pulled up to the newsroom building across from the main studios, Warren Fulks, our ten o'clock newscaster, rushed out to meet me, shouting, "The president's been shot and taken to Parkland!"

"Grab a camera, Abe," I said, "and let's go." Warren Fulks had the noble stature of a lean and rangy Abraham Lincoln, hence the nickname. Abe was a solid journalist and a naturally dramatic newscaster. He and I were young, eager and shaken, and I took us up Harry Hines Boulevard with my foot on the floor. I approached an empty cardboard box in the road and rammed it aside, then reached Parkland seconds after police guards had blocked all entrances. Trusting the power of the press card on the windshield, I bypassed the cordoned entrances, drove the wagon over the curb, then jumped medians all the way across the parking lot to the back of the hospital. I parked as near the emergency room as guards would allow, about 150 feet from the president's bloodied limousine, standing with its doors still ajar. Dignitaries who had been in the motorcade were milling there in a daze.

Senator Ralph Yarborough, whose liberal estrangement from LBJ's powerful conservative Democrats was behind JFK's Texas junket, had been riding reluctantly with his nemesis and Lady Bird Johnson in an open car not far behind the president's. Yarborough stared at me in disbelief and said, "It sounded like a fusillade of shots." In the previous day's Houston motorcade he had declined to ride with LBJ, and before leaving Fort Worth that morning, President Kennedy had approached Governor Connally with the problem.

"John, did you know that Yarborough wouldn't ride with Johnson yesterday?"

"Yes, sir."

"Well, he's going to ride with him today, or he's going to walk."

Back at the scene of the shooting, my colleague Jim Underwood, who had been in an open press car close behind the limo bearing LBJ and Yarborough, had vaulted out of the convertible at the sound of three shots from overhead. An alert Marine veteran, Jim had been in the thick of the Guadalcanal invasion, and he kept his wits. When JFK's Lincoln braked hard, then screamed away onto Stemmons Freeway, Jim ran with police as they combed railyards above the triple underpass. He joined officers converging on the Texas School Book Depository, then raced to a telephone to make the first report. Underwood, KRLD's assistant news director, had a combat rifleman's sense for the direction of sniper fire. Gasping for breath, he made this live report:

> As the car I was in made the turn at Elm and Houston and started down for the triple underpass, I heard three loud shots seemingly from right over my head. There was so much confusion with people running, I thought at first that some of the spectators farther down the street toward the Elm Street underpass had been hit. I saw many of them throw themselves flat on the ground, and the police officers started blowing whistles and running for the scene. I leaped out of the car I was in in the parade and ran for the scene also.

As sirens screamed and police surrounded the area, Jim said, "Evidently police believe that the man who fired the shots is still in the Texas School Book Depository building at the corner of Elm and Houston in downtown Dallas."

VIGIL AT THE EMERGENCY ROOM

At Parkland, Warren and I waited to learn how seriously the shooting had wounded the president and governor. I knew that Jay Hogan, at our newsroom controls, was busy following the search for the gunman, so I started making my reports directly through the main radio control room across the street. Knowing that we had to stay on the air to reassure listeners even when we had nothing new to report, I keyed the mike and told the announcer and engineer, "Keep us on and tape everything we do." We had to record history.

Warren Fulks and I stayed on the air with as much information and description as we could glean, alternating between the mobile unit's hand mike and the press briefings that Assistant Press Secretary Malcolm Kil-duff would soon begin holding inside the hospital. One reason for stay-ing on the air even without new information was to assure people that we were there to tell them the story as it developed. Another reason was to keep summarizing the sad sequence of events for those just tuning in.

To stay on the air, we had to have the station wagon on the scene, and we were bound to the mobile unit, our only way of broadcasting without telephone connections. We kept fingers pressed to the mike's talk but-ton, or else the hiss of the squelch breaking would intrude on the broad-cast. Since we were using our only two-way frequency, we couldn't talk to our studios or newsroom while we were on the air.

I walked through the stunned group and spoke in hushed tones with legislators who replied as they brushed aside tears. A pair of priests hur-ried past me toward the emergency room doors. Dreading what I had to say, I returned to the car, radioed the studios to put me on, took the cue through my transistor radio and began.

> What was a wonderful welcome in downtown Dallas has become a scene of indescribable horror, as hundreds of people crowd outside the back door to the emergency room here at Parkland Hospital. Faces are ashen white. And people are wondering, 'Is our president going to live?' President Kennedy is on the inside of Parkland Hospital, and two priests have just been sent into the room with the president.

I reported that Congressman Jim Wright had said that he heard three shots and that Senator Yarborough had told me that he believed the president's injuries to be very grave. "Reporters are being held outside the back door of Parkland Hospital, awaiting some announcement, some word on the condition of the president." I handed Warren the mike, and he continued.

> All we can add at this time is that about three and a half minutes ago a spokesman from the hospital addressed himself to the press corps behind the hospital near the emergency exit, saying he could not elab-orate on the extent of the president's injuries or the location of those injuries. Yarborough, who was riding I believe some two cars behind that of the president, was visibly shaken. He said the scene was too horrible to describe. However, we must bear in mind that he himself,

Senator Ralph Yarborough, who rode with Vice President Lyndon Johnson two cars behind JFK's, talks to reporters at Parkland. George Phenix in left background. *Photograph courtesy The Sixth Floor Museum at Dealey Plaza.* Dallas Times Herald *Collection*

being an eyewitness, was very visibly disturbed and is as confused here as anyone else is. We are here at the scene, and we will remain here at Parkland Hospital.

Warren headed inside the hospital to a first-floor room where Malcolm Kilduff was starting to deal with converging reporters. Our colleague George Phenix had caught a ride from the Trade Mart to Parkland and was filming the scene inside and outside the building. Our reporter Dan Garza was on his way with another wagon and fresh film. We knew that Parkland Hospital had one of the nation's busiest trauma centers and a staff of its top surgeons. If anyone could save gunshot victims, Parkland trauma teams could, and we were praying that they would.

WAITING AT THE TRADE MART

I went on interviewing dignitaries in the motorcade's remnants and staying by our mobile unit to feed more reports and listen to those coming from my colleagues. Wes Wise had gone from his Lemmon Avenue motorcade broadcast straight to the Trade Mart. Sitting with his wife, Sally, Wes had been a guest. Now on the air, he was a reporter again:

> The first inkling of what has happened leaked into the Trade Mart as police and Secret Service men, then newsmen and photographers following close by, began running about the four balconies of the huge Trade Mart building. Up until a few moments ago, perhaps no more than fifty or sixty people in the huge crowd of some three thousand knew what has happened. Then I hurried to this phone. People who recognized me from local television called out to me as I ran by, "Is it true? Is it true?"

Wes described the anguished guests: women with tear-stained cheeks, elderly men with heads bowed to the tables where they sat, the ominous public-address announcement of a delay, the unexplained request that people stay seated.

At Dealey Plaza, our assignments editor, Joe Scott, was standing outside the School Book Depository. Small, dour and skeptical, Joe usually kept his distance from microphones. He and our Fort Worth reporter, Steve Pieringer, were using Steve's mobile unit to broadcast. This was the only time I ever heard Joe on the air: "We're down here at the scene of the current manhunt. There must be over two dozen squad cars blocking the intersection of Elm and Houston Streets." Joe had been shooting film at Love Field with Pieringer, and the two of them had headed for the action when police monitors in Steve's mobile unit had alerted them to the shots at Dealey Plaza. "So far," Joe reported, "no one has been apprehended, but more than a score of Dallas policemen are standing with shotguns poised on their hip, ready and looking upward."

Steve Pieringer covered Fort Worth and the Tarrant County area with a station wagon so overspread with antennae that I teased him about its looking like an inverted hairbrush. Our newsroom and most of our mobile units monitored several Dallas police, sheriff, and fire frequencies, but Steve had outfitted his Pontiac also to receive everything throughout Fort Worth and Tarrant County. Eddie staffed the department with

Shotguns outside the Texas School Book Depository moments after JFK's assassination. *Photograph courtesy The Sixth Floor Museum at Dealey Plaza.* Dallas Times Herald *Collection*

men who wrote, shot 16 mm movie film, reported news of all kinds, and in the face of this disastrous story, knew where to go and what to do. They were moving on their own. At the School Book Depository, Joe handed the mike to Steve, who reported discoveries inside the building: "Jerry Hill of the Dallas Police Department just leaned out a window and told police to call the Dallas crime laboratory to the scene. Apparently they've found some shells there in that room in the Texas School Book Depository building. Other police officers currently have the scene surrounded, while still more with shotguns are searching out the building at this time."

Inside the surrounded building, police were leading the depository's management in accounting for their employees. One worker, Lee Oswald, was missing. It was his thirty-ninth day as an order clerk there, and he'd been seen on the sixth floor half an hour before the shooting, then below in the lunchroom within a couple of minutes after he'd pulled the trigger.

Oswald had abandoned the rifle that he'd sneaked into the building that morning packaged as what he'd claimed were curtain rods. After the shooting, he had passed through the lunchroom, gone out the front

After discovery of three spent cartridges on the sixth floor, Sergeant Jerry Hill calls down for the crime lab. *Photograph courtesy The Sixth Floor Museum at Dealey Plaza*. Dallas Times Herald *Collection*

door, made his way through the confusion, and walked east on Elm Street toward the heart of downtown. After seven blocks, he knocked on the door of a westbound Oak Cliff bus, boarded it and headed back toward the depository. Two blocks and four minutes later he changed his mind, had a transfer punched, and got off the bus just ahead of snarled traffic at Dealey Plaza. He walked south to the Greyhound bus station on Lamar and climbed into one of the taxis at curbside there.

While investigators in the building were discovering his absence, Oswald was in the cab, westbound across the Trinity River to his rented room in Oak Cliff. He was in a hurry to get the pistol that he kept there, and soon he would use it to take another life that day.

At Parkland the terrible dream would not end. Legislators behind the presidential limousine in the motorcade had been basking in cheers and confetti—then, their leader killed by Oswald's old Italian rifle, had sped up Stemmons Freeway in wild flight, sirens screaming to the emergency door, JFK's open car soaked with gore and Jackie's red roses on the floorboard with her husband's blood. The party of surviving politicians were shattered, and I questioned them with gentleness. Congressman Ray Roberts stared at the ground shaking his head: "I simply couldn't say anything. I simply couldn't tell you anything. I just can't think straight."

While I scraped for more information, Warren was inside waiting for a briefing, and I had to keep reporting: "The crowd is growing as spectators who have just learned of the horrible thing that has happened are sifting in from the street—walking in. People of all descriptions are standing here behind Parkland Hospital and waiting for some iota, some word about the condition of the president."

As I spoke again to Senator Ralph Yarborough, he burst into tears and told me, "I saw a Secret Service man on the rear of the presidential car and pounding it with his hands in despair, anguish, and pain. I knew something horrible had happened."

"The first lady is in the emergency room with the president," I reported, "and the crowd outside is quiet and waiting for some word on his condition."

At the Trade Mart, luncheon guests began to suspect the worst. Wes continued radio broadcasts from there by telephone, and Eddie Barker used KRLD's waiting pool camera connection to feed live television: "The only thing that we have at this time is the report that the president is at Parkland Hospital, that Governor John Connally was also wounded."

Eddie paused as the minister who was to have given the luncheon's invocation stepped to the dais. Eddie, who knew the community's leaders well, spoke low into his broadcast mike as he introduced the Reverend Luther Holcomb, executive secretary of the Dallas Council of Churches. Then Eddie fell silent as the minister, speaking over the public address system, prayed for the wounded chief executives and their families. Behind the blurred audio of the minister's prayer, one could hear Eddie breathing. After the amen, he continued, "The shots apparently came from the Texas School Book Depository, which is a building about eight floors in height that—yes?" Again he paused, as a man approached him and whispered, "Eddie, he's dead." Barker listened while holding his mike away from the informant, then asked, "And who are you, sir?"

"I don't want to be identified," the man replied, and Eddie went on in a tone of despair: "We have just been told by a member of the staff at Parkland Hospital, the president is dead. This is not—what is the governor's condition?"

"He's been shot in the chest."

"In the chest. Do you have any report on that?"

"No, no."

Eddie gave the nation the tragic news: "The word we have is that President Kennedy is dead. This we do not know for a fact. The word we have is that he is dead, that he was shot by an assassin at the intersection of Elm and Houston Streets just as he was going into the underpass. The word we have is from a doctor on the staff at Parkland Hospital who says that it is true. He was in tears when he told me just a moment ago."

Ever the professional, Eddie went on giving as much information as he had, describing the president's entire Texas visit that had begun in San Antonio and Houston the day before. The president and his party had stayed overnight at Fort Worth's Hotel Texas. Early that fateful morning JFK had walked into a crowd of several thousand in a downtown Fort Worth parking lot. Eddie mentioned fears that right-wing demonstrators might have spoiled the president's welcome at Dallas Love Field. "But nothing went wrong there," he continued. "There were some pickets, there were some demonstrators, but the president in his charming manner moved into the crowd with his wife by his side and greeted and shook hands."

Eddie even summarized the unexpected weather, which had begun gray and cold in Dallas that morning, then turned to a beautiful sunny day that had perhaps changed history. The morning fog, rain, and low clouds had been forecast to continue through the afternoon, but the overcast had broken away. "And when the president's big jet set down right on schedule at twenty-five minutes before the noon hour, Central time, the sun was bright, the crowds were out, the bubble Plexiglas cover for the president's limousine was put away, and the president and his wife and the governor of the state of Texas rode in the open car."

Eddie's reporting under such anguish was controlled and complete. He had judged his source on the spot and had the courage to break the terrible news. The first to announce the president's death, he had overcome his grief to tell of the governor's chest wound, then to summarize JFK's Texas visit and show how unexpectedly fine weather had exposed the riders in the open car: if morning rain had continued as forecast, the bubble top, although not bulletproof, might have deflected Oswald's shots.

President Kennedy had told Jackie that morning, "You know, last night would have been a hell of a night to assassinate a president. I mean it. There was the rain and the night, and we were all being jostled. Suppose a man had a pistol in a briefcase."

In the emergency room, Dr. Malcolm Perry had performed a tracheotomy through the exit wound in the president's throat in a futile effort to revive him. He and Dr. Robert McClelland tried despite the hopelessness of Kennedy's massive head wound. JFK had been dead on arrival, but they took heroic measures in Trauma Room One while other doctors were attending the wounded governor.

JIM WRIGHT'S PRAYER

Outside the hospital Congressman Jim Wright was standing beside me at the mobile unit when we learned that JFK was dead. I had intended to ask the future House Speaker more about what he had seen and heard during the shooting, but when we learned the awful news, grief overcame us, and I said, "No one wants to say anything on an occasion like this. But someone must have something to say. We have with us

Fort Worth Congressman Jim Wright. Mr. Wright, do you have something to say?"

I held the mike for him as Jim Wright bowed his head:

> We have just learned that our president is dead. This is a sad day—a
> day of grief, a day of shame for this land that anyone would hate, that
> anyone would seek to kill the president of the United States. We must
> strive anew to rebuild our faith and our hope. May a merciful God con-
> sole his loved ones and his family. May that same God bless this land,
> that from this moment of such deep grief we may rebuild in faith, and
> not in fear—and love, and not in hate. I know the nation mourns and
> will deeply mourn. Those of us who were with him today when he was
> so alive, so buoyant, so outgoing, exposing himself to the public, will
> never forget this experience and will always remember him as the pres-
> ident who went to the people, not fearing to expose himself—his per-
> son, his safety, his own repose—to his land and his people. It is tragic
> that in this free land anyone would so learn to hate in his heart that he
> would seek to take violently into his hands this kind of an act. But it has
> been done. There is still in this land the fiber to rebuild on a basis of re-
> spect for duly constituted authority. And we must do it, and we must
> not panic.

In Oak Cliff, Lee Oswald was telling the cab driver where to drop him
off. The assassin was only twenty-four. He had a childhood obsession
with the television series *I Led Three Lives,* and he was behaving like a
bumbling version of his double-agent heroes. The previous April he had
told his Russian wife, Marina, that he had taken a shot with his rifle at
the ultraconservative Major General Edwin A. Walker, a fervent enemy
of JFK. Firing in darkness as Walker sat in his study, Oswald had hit a
window frame. He had missed a serious shot at the rabid right-winger,
then killed the left-leaning president. Oswald's pattern didn't seem to
make sense—unless, perhaps, he was emulating a double agent. But despite his attraction to communism, he had failed to establish himself in
either Russia or Cuba, and the U.S. president symbolized the native land
he had come to hate.

Without betraying his destination, he guided the cabbie a block past
the single-story house at 1026 North Beckley. He gave the driver a dol-
lar for the ninety-five-cent fare, turned, walked back and rushed into

the house where his landlady, who knew him as "O. H. Lee," remarked on his strange hurry as she watched his tragedy unfolding on television. In his room he slipped into a jacket, tucked the pistol beneath it, then left the house and set out on foot.

Discovering within minutes that Oswald was the only employee missing from the depository, at 12:45 police began broadcasting his description every few minutes to all units. Only fifteen minutes had passed since he'd fired the rifle. Beside the sixth-floor window in his nest of boxes, police would find three spent shells and the long paper bag that had encased his "curtain rods." Soon they would discover the rifle he had concealed among boxes near the stairway on his way down. Later they would find prints of his fingers and hands on those boxes and bag—and his palm print on the rifle stock. Patrol cars already were scouring Oak Cliff for a white male, about thirty, five-foot-ten, 165 pounds. Initial police radio reports had said that he might be armed—with a rifle.

At Parkland I was reporting from a crowd gone silent except for muffled sobbing: "People are standing outside this emergency entrance to the hospital and weeping bitterly. Senator Ralph Yarborough, Congressman Ray Roberts, Congressman Olin Teague of the Sixth District—all are crying. None can express what they feel. The only question that remains in most of their minds, all they can say now is, 'How is John?' They mean, of course, Governor John Connally." I reported that the governor had been shot in the upper right chest, and I described the terrible scene that remains seared into my memory, as the crowd awaited more news of the tragedy.

"The crowd waits with disbelief in their eyes. People are crying all around us. Newsmen who see death every day are crying, congressmen, senators who loved the president: a scene of indescribable sadness and horror at the emergency entrance to Parkland Hospital."

Inside the hospital, Lyndon Johnson was under guard. When doctors told Malcolm Kilduff that the president was dead, the assistant press secretary had entered LBJ's secure room and addressed him as "Mr. President." At those chilling words Lady Bird, standing beside her towering husband, had suppressed a little scream. Johnson started giving orders: "There's a conspiracy. Get me out to Air Force One."

The nation's military went to high alert, and heavily armed officers stood at the end of the Love Field flight path to guard Air Force One's takeoff. On Johnson's orders, attendants closed and curtained the big

The sniper's nest where Oswald fired, hidden by boxes that he had stacked.
Photograph courtesy The Sixth Floor Museum at Dealey Plaza. Photographer William Allen. Dallas Times Herald *Collection*

The box positioned approximately where Oswald rested his rifle for clear shots at the rear of the presidential limousine. *Photograph courtesy The Sixth Floor Museum at Dealey Plaza. Photographer William Allen.* Dallas Times Herald *Collection*

liner's windows. Federal Judge Sarah T. Hughes headed from the forlorn and aborted Trade Mart luncheon to swear in the new president aboard the plane. Technicians removed and stowed a bulkhead and some seats to accommodate JFK's casket.

In our newsroom, Jay Hogan was updating the chain of events and switching between CBS and our local reports. By telephone he questioned Mary Moorman, who had witnessed from the curb as the shots struck their mark:

"About how close were you?"

"Fifteen foot. I know, 'cause that's where I had my camera set."

"This was right at the underpass?"

"Yes, just a few feet from the underpass."

"Were you up on that grassy bank there?"

"Yes, that's where we were, and I'd stepped out in the street. We were right at the car."

"How many shots did you hear? You say shots rang out."

"Oh, I don't know—I think three or four is what I heard. It just took seconds for me to realize what was happening."

"What was your first thought?"

"That those are shots—and that he has been hit. And that they're liable to hit me 'cause I'm right at the car. So I decided that the place for me was to just get on the ground. He grabbed his chest, and of course Mrs. Kennedy jumped up immediately and fell over him. And she says, 'My God, he's been shot!'"

"Did you notice any other reactions of persons around the president in the motorcade there at the time of the shots?"

"They hesitated just for a moment, 'cause I think they were like I was, you know: was that a shot or was it a backfire or just what? And then, 'course, he clutched his chest, and they immediately sped up. Real fast, you know, like, getting out of there. And, of the police, there were several motorcycles around him, and they stopped, and one or two must have went with him, and one ran up the hill."

The unexpected sunshine was brilliant, and the cold and drizzly autumn morning had given way to a balmy noon. Under blue skies, sun had glinted from the president's polished limousine. Jackie Kennedy, smiling as the motorcade began, had put on her sunglasses. "Take off your glasses," her husband had said with a smile, as she put on her best face for miles of crowds lining the curbs.

She, Jack, and the Connallys had been beaming and brushing away confetti as the big Lincoln turned right onto Houston Street in Dealey Plaza, facing the Texas School Book Depository. Nellie Connally had turned and said, "Mr. President, you can't say Dallas doesn't love you!"

At KRLD's radio news desk, Jay Hogan went on interviewing witnesses. Having spoken to Mary Moorman, Jay questioned Jean Hill, Mary's friend who had been with her near the limousine when the bullets hit their target.

"Miss Hill, you were an eyewitness also?"

"Yes I was. I suppose we were the people closest to the president's car at the time."

"That was about ten or fifteen feet, you say?"

"Not any more than that at all."

"You were both looking right at the presidential car, then?"

"Yes, we were looking right at the president. We were looking in his face. As Mary took the picture, I was looking at him. And when two shots rang out, he grabbed his hands across his chest, and—I'd never seen anyone killed or in pain before like that, but there was this odd look came across his face, and he pitched forward onto Jackie's lap. And she fell across him and said, 'My God, he's been shot.'"

Seconds later Jackie Kennedy had said, "My God, I've got his brains in my hand." And as the driver slowed the big car, the first lady had crawled out onto its rear deck to reach for the hand of JFK's foiled Secret Service guard when he climbed in as they sped away.

2

Murderous Flight

BOB HUFFAKER

Across the Trinity now, his snub-nosed revolver under his light gray jacket, Lee Oswald was in a hurry. Leaving his room, he walked southward for a few blocks and turned onto Tenth Street, traveling east through a neighborhood of forty-year-old houses. A hundred feet or so past Patton Avenue, a police car driven by officer J. D. Tippit, a handsome, wavy-haired veteran on the Oak Cliff beat, overtook the young gunman as he quickened his steps down the south side of Tenth.

The radio dispatcher's description of Oswald hadn't warned Unit 78 of that concealed pistol. The patrolman pulled next to the curb, leaned across and hailed Oswald through the passenger window. Witnesses watched as Oswald stopped, approached the window, and talked with Tippit.

Something in that short conversation made the officer get out on his side of the car and walk around its front toward Oswald. Onlookers were aghast to see the fugitive blow Tippit down with three shots to the chest, then stand over the thirty-nine-year-old father of three and shoot him again in the right temple before reversing his former direction and setting out at a trot toward Jefferson Boulevard's business district a block away. A dozen witnesses saw him emptying the Smith & Wesson .38 of spent cartridges as he fled. He tossed two of the empty shells into nearby bushes as he cleared the gun for reloading.

Taxi driver William Scoggins had been eating lunch in his cab, parked on Patton facing the southeast corner of its intersection with Tenth. When he saw the killer headed toward him with the revolver, he ducked out of the car and hid behind it. Oswald passed within twelve feet of him, close enough for Scoggins to hear him mutter, "Poor damn cop" or perhaps "dumb cop."

As Oswald started running, Domingo Benavides rose from where he had flattened himself below his pickup's window. He saw the killer toss two empty cartridges into shrubbery. Benavides had been driving west on Tenth toward Tippit's patrol car when he saw the killing from thirty feet away, stopped the truck and dived for cover on its floorboards. He climbed out to help the fallen officer as Oswald ran back down the block toward Scoggins' taxi.

Helen Markham, a downtown waitress, had seen the entire drama from the northwest corner of Tenth and Patton as she was about to cross the intersection. She ran to the patrol car and screamed as she looked down at J. D. Tippit lying in a pool of his blood.

Inside their apartment house on the southeast corner, Barbara and Virginia Davis heard her scream and ran to the door in time to see Oswald shake the last two casings from the open cylinder as he cut across their yard.

While others were arriving, all too late to save Tippit, Benavides opened the door of the dead man's black Ford and handed its dash-mounted microphone to Thomas Bowley, who used its radio to call for help at 1:18: "Hello, police operator?"

"Go ahead. Go ahead, citizen using a police radio," the dispatcher responded.

"We've had a shooting out here."

"Where's it at?" the dispatcher asked. "The citizen using police radio?"

"On Tenth Street."

"What location on Tenth Street?"

"Between Marsalis and Beckley. It's a police officer. Somebody shot him! What's this—404 Tenth Street."

"Seventy-eight," the dispatcher called the officer who now lay dead.

"You got that?" Bowley said into Tippit's mike. "It's in a police car, number ten. You got that?"

"Seventy-eight?" The dispatcher again called in vain to the patrolman who'd driven Car 10. Then the dispatcher broadcast a signal nineteen—a shooting—involving a police officer.

When other patrol officers arrived, Domingo Benavides showed them where Oswald had discarded two of the shell casings, and he

Officer J. D. Tippit's patrol car remains where he had stopped it to question Oswald. *Photograph courtesy The Sixth Floor Museum at Dealey Plaza. Photographer Darryl Heikes.* Dallas Times Herald *Collection*

helped them find the hulls in the bushes. Barbara and Virginia Davis found the other two where they'd seen Oswald shake them out of the cylinder.

A block away, Oswald shed his jacket behind a gas station and tossed it under a parked car, then tried to blend in with shoppers along busy Jefferson Boulevard as the police dispatcher broadcast, "The subject's running west on Jefferson from the location."

Police cars converged up and down the street, and Oswald pretended to look at shop displays in showcase alcoves. To avoid the increasing police traffic, the desperate assassin slipped into Hardy's Shoe Store. Johnny Brewer, the manager, noticed how Oswald cringed and averted his face when patrol cars passed. He was suspicious of the shifty and rumpled young man, and when Oswald left, Brewer stepped out of his store and watched the killer hurry four doors down and duck into the Texas Theater. Brewer walked to the box office and asked the cashier, Julia Postal, whether that guy had bought a ticket. "As a matter of fact, he didn't," she said, and Brewer went into the theater while she dialed police.

At the third row from the back of the darkened theater, Oswald had taken the fifth seat from the right center aisle. The Friday matinee was a double feature: *Cry of Battle* and *War Is Hell*. He sat tight while movie gunfire roared on the screen. *War Is Hell* was playing as he pretended to watch.

THE MOURNFUL BRIEFING

At Parkland, Assistant Press Secretary Malcolm Kilduff finished his last sad briefing. Then Governor Connally's spokesman Bill Stinson gave us word on the governor's condition. I took my notes outside to the car, where Warren Fulks, aka Abe, handed me the mike and asked, "What have you got?" He was grabbing his note pad off the front seat.

"Finally got Connally's wounds. Chest. Up high and probably from behind. Pretty bad, but he's probably going to make it."

Abe shook his head, fished a pen out of his shirt pocket, then headed back inside to the room I'd just left. I called the studios and went back on the air: "We're speaking once again from Parkland Hospital and have just come from the temporary press room which has been set up here in the south side of the building. Briefing the press in this most distasteful session was administrative aide to Governor Connally Bill Stinson. This is the first report, and the latest, on Governor Connally's condition. He has been shot in the upper right chest, and his body is completely perforated." I told of the governor's broken wrist, which at that time was a wound that Secret Servicemen had been unable to explain, beyond speculating that it might have come from another bullet or from Connally's struggle to survive. Stinson had told me that when the governor was first brought into the emergency room, he'd asked him, "How bad are you?" and Connally had told him that he thought he'd been hit from the back. Stinson, my only official source then on the governor's condition, had described it as very serious, but with great hope. I relayed his information about Connally's strong vital signs as Parkland surgeons worked inside to save him. I concluded, "Both Mrs. Connally and Mrs. Kennedy are uninjured. They're OK."

Leaving Stinson's briefing moments before, I had passed Malcolm Kilduff, JFK's acting press secretary on the Texas tour. Most reporters had already rushed from the makeshift press room in search of telephones, and Kilduff was still standing at the front of the room. We

Assistant Press Secretary Malcolm Kilduff announces the president's death at
Parkland Hospital. *Photograph courtesy The Sixth Floor Museum at Dealey Plaza.*
Dallas Times Herald *Collection*

looked at each other in benumbed silence; then he stared at the floor
as he said, "This is one briefing I never thought I'd give."

THE INCOMPETENT ASSASSIN

In the Texas Theater Lee Oswald was sitting alone while the screen's
cinematic battles cast reflections on his pallid face. He obviously had
not planned his escape before pulling the trigger, and he couldn't slip
the inexorable tightening noose as police moved to ensnare him. He
had botched his getaway at every turn—abandoning his rifle at the
scene with a live round still inside, bailing out of a stranded bus, creeping through snarled traffic in a cab, murdering a policeman before witnesses, trying to hide on one of Oak Cliff's busiest streets, then sitting
in a movie unaware that his uneasy behavior had betrayed him. He'd
blown his cover in the shoe store, and he might have guessed that the
box-office clerk would notice when he didn't stop to pay. He was bet-
ting a long shot and pretending to watch the screen.

Dallas cops had a reputation for amazingly short response times, and
within minutes they descended on Oswald like ducks on a June bug.

Sergeant Jerry Hill, in plain clothes, had called for the crime lab to come to the sniper's sixth-floor nest at the School Book Depository, then had gone to the scene of J.D. Tippit's murder, then to the theater, where two officers were already posted out front with shotguns. When Patrolman Nick McDonald and other officers had arrived, Johnny Brewer, the shoe store manager, had accompanied them into the theater. As war continued in black and white, management brought up the house lights. In the balcony, Jerry Hill kicked open the fire doors to admit more light. Brewer stood on stage and in an undertone indicated Oswald to the cops.

Nick McDonald moved from beside the stage into the audience and made a pretense of searching a couple of patrons near the front. Advancing with care, he tried to keep his quarry off guard. Looking away from Oswald, the burly policeman walked up the right center aisle, his pistol still holstered. Oswald shifted his position as the officer approached, taking the second seat from the aisle. McDonald drew up beside Oswald, turned and said, "On your feet."

Oswald stood and said, "This is it!" As McDonald reached to search near the Smith & Wesson at his waist, the assassin punched the officer with a left between the eyes and drew the pistol with his right hand. McDonald wrestled with Oswald and grasped the revolver with his left. Jerry Hill had just come back down into the lobby after searching the balcony when he heard the commotion and rushed into the fray. McDonald held the cylinder tight as he felt the hammer snap against the skin between his thumb and forefinger, softening its impact enough to stop the firing pin from doing its job. McDonald's hat fell off as he wrenched the short-barreled pistol to the side. He and Jerry Hill fought Oswald down into the seats, as Patrolman Tommy Hudson piled on. Several other cops jumped into the wild struggle as Oswald fought bitterly. They wrestled for control of the pistol, then at last disarmed him before he could get off a shot. McDonald got a deep scratch down his face, and Oswald's left eye was swelling as they hustled him out of the theater yelling, "I protest this police brutality!" It had been one hell of a fight, and nobody was sure just how the scratches and bruises happened.

Detective Bob Carroll had emerged from the tussle with Oswald's pistol. He and his partner, Kenneth Lyons, climbed into the front seat of Carroll's car along with Jerry Hill. Detective Paul Bentley and Patrolman C. T. Walker sandwiched Oswald between them in the back seat. They

Officer Nick McDonald, face scratched, tells *Dallas Morning News* reporter Jim Ewell
of Oswald's arrest. *Photograph courtesy The Sixth Floor Museum at Dealey Plaza.*
Tom Dillard Collection, Dallas Morning News

knew only that they had Tippit's killer in custody as they drove to headquarters with the man who had also killed the president.

Jim Underwood, alerted by police radio transmissions, was among
the few reporters who met them at the Police and Courts Building, and
he filmed the officers hustling Oswald up the elevator to the homicide
office.

Sergeant Jerry Hill was a regular around our newsroom, where he reported on traffic and worked closely with us. Detective Bob Carroll
handed him Oswald's pistol, which Jerry had to hang onto until he could
get it on its way through channels to the crime lab. They sat Oswald
down in the homicide interrogation room, and Jerry was sitting beside
its door when Will Fritz, the teddy-bearish and grandfatherly captain of

homicide and robbery, returned from the School Book Depository. Fritz instructed two of his detectives, Gus Rose and Richard Stovall, to go and search the Irving home of Ruth Paine, where Oswald's wife lived, and to arrest Lee Harvey Oswald, the absent depository worker, on suspicion of killing the president.

"You don't need to go out there to get him," Jerry told the captain.

"Why?" Fritz asked, and Jerry gestured toward the interrogation room.

"'Cause there the son of a bitch sits."

Typing the mandatory report on injury to the suspect, Jerry Hill had described Oswald as a suspect only in Tippit's shooting, then had to revise the subject line to read, "Injury while effecting the arrest of the suspect in the assassination of the president of the United States and the murder of Officer J. D. Tippit."

LEAVING FOR WASHINGTON

Aboard Air Force One at Love Field, Judge Sarah T. Hughes had just sworn in Lyndon Johnson as the late president's successor, and LBJ was eager to get that big jet off the ground and on its way to Washington. On Johnson's order, Secret Servicemen at Parkland had already removed the president's body after some tense moments when the Dallas County medical examiner, Dr. Earl Rose, had tried to hold the corpse for the autopsy and murder investigation. The feds and the locals had engaged in a brief tug of war with the casket, almost jostling off the crucifix that lay on its top.

Outside, federal agents and a contingent of police began clearing the area around the emergency entrance, and they told me that I must move the mobile unit. Jim Wright, Ralph Yarborough, and other legislators had to move away too. We were quiet and cooperative as grim Secret Service agents pushed us all back a hundred yards from the rear entrance. No one told us what was happening, but we knew. People who had walked into the parking area from the street stared toward the rear of the hospital, and I stood beside the station wagon, my spiral mike cord pulled through its window. I gave the saddest report of my life:

> For a number of hours this afternoon the door has been ringed with newsmen and anxious spectators. Not too long ago, when the announcement was made that John F. Kennedy had died of the assassin's

Police carry Oswald's makeshift rifle bag from the School Book Depository. *Times-Herald* reporter Darwin Payne at extreme right. *Photograph courtesy The Sixth Floor Museum at Dealey Plaza. Photographer William Allen.* Dallas Times Herald *Collection*

bullet, people stood for several more minutes in disbelief. Many are still standing, now at a greater distance from the hospital, having been moved back by Secret Service agents and Dallas police. There are still a number of congressmen seated in cars. Few can find the words to describe what they feel at this time.

There is a flurry of movement now. And from the rear of the hospital comes first the lead police car and two following motorcycles. Here comes a white hearse, leaving the hospital followed by cars full of Secret Servicemen and one last motorcycle.

And now that the hearse has passed, the crowd is breaking up. And people are wandering away, still wondering, still shocked. Some are weeping; some are in dead silence. This is one of the quietest crowds that will ever assemble—the crowd with pity, sorrow, horror, and shame in its heart. For this was the day that the president of the United States died from an assassin's bullet in Dallas, Texas.

I hated having to speak when I felt like weeping. Warren and I made a last round at the hospital. The somber crowd had dispersed. Billie,

The crowd outside Parkland Hospital learns of the president's death. *Photograph courtesy The Sixth Floor Museum at Dealey Plaza. Photographer Eamon Kennedy.* Dallas Times Herald *Collection*

The silent crowd at Parkland hears that JFK is dead. *Photograph courtesy The Sixth Floor Museum at Dealey Plaza. Photographer Eamon Kennedy.* Dallas Times Herald *Collection*

my tough old contact at the emergency room desk, later told me that the president had been DOA. I radioed the newsroom that we were coming back, and Abe settled into the passenger seat and bent over his notes as I drove southward to the station.

Inside the newsroom Jay Hogan was still doing radio newscasts, and Warren and I went to our typewriters. The room was full and busy. Dan Rather, who had been waiting thirty yards past Dealey Plaza for his crew's last film drop on the parade route, had raced five blocks to the station when the stricken motorcade sped past. Dan had skirted the confusion in the streets to reach our communications base, where he had confirmed JFK's death with calls to Parkland. Warren and I took calls from other CBS affiliate stations and fed them reports while we wrote for both radio and TV.

Our reporter Dick Wheeler was at police headquarters using a telephone to make radio reports on Oswald and his rifle. Eddie also had sent our television crews there from the Trade Mart, and Bill Mercer was broadcasting through the long evening there as our cameras showed the rifle and its owner being shuttled to and from the third-floor homicide offices.

Sergeant Jerry Hill tells Bill Mercer of subduing Oswald.
Photograph courtesy The Sixth Floor Museum at Dealey Plaza.
Dallas Times Herald *Collection*

The pool camera arrangements had ended, and the three networks were depending on capabilities of their local affiliates. Our two KRLD vans were equipped to broadcast Dallas Cowboy games with several cameras. Our engineers and production people had brought the smaller one, known as "The Bread Truck," to the building, where they pulled cables to position a live camera in the crowded third-floor hallway, another on the basement level, and another outside on Commerce Street. WBAP's mobile van, also akin to a bread truck, wasn't running, so the Fort Worth station had a wrecker tow it all the way to Dallas police headquarters to feed NBC from there.

Dan Rather and his CBS crew were working out of our newsroom, and Dan sent his reporter Lew Wood to Parkland and his other, Nelson Benton, to join Bill Mercer that evening at police headquarters.

Patterning KRLD News on the structure of a network operation, Eddie had built it into one of the best. We were proud of our links to CBS, and like other affiliate stations, when our local news became of national interest we fed reports to CBS News and to other CBS stations. Eddie maintained friendly terms with Walter Cronkite, and we gave CBS correspondents access to our local contacts—and space in our newsroom when they needed it.

A year earlier, while I was at KBTX-TV in Bryan, I had worked with Rather and hosted his crew in my office while we covered a politically charged murder case. Since then, Dan had become the CBS Southwest bureau chief—a familiar face in our KRLD newsroom, although the network had recently moved his headquarters from Dallas to New Orleans.

We wrote our own copy. There were no news readers among us. Eddie demanded versatility, and all of us were prepared to report and write as well as shoot film and operate audio equipment. Video—as opposed to our 16 mm newsfilm—was the purview of our engineering and production people. There were no tape cassettes or cartridges in those days, and both video and audio were recorded on reel-to-reel devices. Videotape machines weren't yet portable. The size of big deep freezers, they were either installed in a studio or mounted in a van, using reels of tape two inches wide.

Outside Captain Will Fritz's office, Bill Mercer was reporting as our live CBS camera showed the tense and raucous scene in the third-floor hallway. Bill was struggling to keep his balance in the increasingly unruly crowd of reporters who were converging from all over the world. Dick

Wheeler was feeding radio reports from the press room down the hall from Captain Friz's homicide office:

> This rifle is of a six-point-five millimeter size . . . believed to have been manufactured about 1940 in Italy. The rifle was a heavy weapon; it had a bolt action, it had a four-power scope mounted on the top of the rifle, and we understand that there was one live round of ammunition found in the rifle when it was recovered from the sixth floor of the building from which the assassination is believed to have taken place. This weapon has not yet been definitely tied in with the suspect who is being held now in jail here and in Captain Fritz's office. He is being taken back and forth. Our District Attorney, Henry Wade, about five minutes ago entered the office of Captain Will Fritz.

At midnight Bill Mercer and his live camera would confront Oswald in a strange impromptu press conference, as police tried to satisfy insistent reporters arriving from all over the world. While the converging press clamored for police to show that they weren't beating Oswald, I was in our newsroom checking Governor Connally's condition every half-hour, updating copy and reporting by phone to other CBS affiliates. Warren Fulks, as usual, put together and delivered the ten o'clock television news. As always, we were mimeographing copies for film editors, directors, and other production staff. Those of us writing for both radio and television were exchanging copies. Behind the mike in our newsroom studio, Jay Hogan was still doing radio news, writing copy, using some of ours, and editing wire stories.

Jay, a scholarly old pro who had directed radio news before Eddie took over the combined radio-TV news operation, was genteel, private, and soft-spoken. His social life was confined to his neighborhood bar, where he drank in moderation. He had a grownup daughter somewhere at a distance, and he kept an old leather-bound copy of Omar Khayyam in a desk drawer.

Well past midnight I went for a few hours' sleep at the apartment I shared with a trucker, a mechanic, and my KRLD News colleague Dean Angel, a wise young gentleman as pure-hearted as his name, who edited film, reported and wrote. Dean had spent the day working with our film chief, Henk Dewit, pushing film through the developers so fast that some of it was streaked. He and I both were sleeping and going back to work with little time for greetings on the way.

Jay Hogan had stuck by the radio desk, and at midnight before he could rest, the old sage ended his last newscast in verse:

> It has all been a long dark night since last Friday,
> And daylight hours are still needed here.
> But Mr. President, may we say one last goodnight,
> When there must be perpetual light
> In your faraway Valhalla, wherever,
> Reserved for souls like yours.
> And we can still see your bright smile
> And your vigorous stride
> Through some mystic Elysian fields.
> Good night, Mr. President—good night.

3

Cables and Carpetbaggers

BOB HUFFAKER

Police headquarters was my regular beat, and Eddie assigned me to join our crews there early on the morning after the assassination. To learn more about police reporting, I'd worked as a part-time cop in the city of Bryan while at the television station there, and our truck-driving apartment mate was a former highway patrolman who had left Brazos County when I had. In Dallas I had built contacts with the police, sheriff's department, fire department, and hospital emergency rooms. I rode on patrol with Sergeant Pat Dean and other Dallas officers, and we drank coffee—and beer when they were off duty. I used a desk in the police press room, and I usually got there before five A.M. and drank nasty black coffee with the *Times-Herald*'s George Carter while we thumbed through overnight complaint forms, better known as "beef sheets."

When I arrived on the morning of Saturday, November 23, the press room was overrun with out-of-town reporters and cluttered with camera equipment, film canisters, extension cords, audiotape recorders, food wrappers and Styrofoam cups. I made the rounds of our mobile van out at the Commerce Street curb and talked to the operators and floor directors running our inside cameras. We stationed one camera in the basement to glimpse Oswald being taken through the jail office. The other remained on the crowded third floor, where reporters were jostling for position in the narrow hallway between the elevators and Captain Fritz's homicide office. I hooked up with Dan Rather's CBS reporter Nelson Benton, a former World War II bomber pilot who proved to be a good friend as he and I took turns with the third-floor camera's mike. Benny Molina, our floor director, and our cameraman, Gene Pasczalek, were wearing headsets that communicated both ways through our vans to CBS's New York studios. The first time Nelson handed me the mike, he said, "If New York calls for you, just give them an update."

Five minutes later Benny said, "New York's coming to you in twenty seconds." The bank of hot lights hit me in the face. Then into the headset, Benny said, "Huffaker. Huff—a—ker," as the New York production people were telling Walter Cronkite how to pronounce my name. "Ten seconds," he told me. "*Huff*-a-ker," he said again. Benny held up five fingers, and five seconds later he pointed to me as the camera's red tally lights blinked on.

I had nothing new to report, but we were trying to assure the world that we were there to tell them as soon as something happened. I summarized the situation, reporting that Fritz intended to continue questioning Oswald soon and that homicide detectives were all over the case: "Here in city hall, tension hangs heavy, and no one knows what is happening behind the closed doors of the homicide office, where officers are working feverishly on the case of President Kennedy's murder." We were reaching the entire nation, and I remembered to specify Central Time as I described events.

Reporters elbowed for position along the hallway, and I was surprised at how rude some were. The assassination was the biggest story of their careers, and visions of Pulitzers danced in their heads. Many of them didn't know the difference between Dallas police and county sheriff deputies. Nor did some of them understand that JFK's assassination was a Texas murder case instead of a federal crime, or why Oswald would be transferred to the county jail after city police had filed charges.

Many reporters came prejudiced against Dallas because its right-wing demonstrators had brutalized Adlai Stevenson the previous month—and because Republican women had jostled Lyndon and Lady Bird Johnson in the Baker Hotel lobby, then spat on them as they crossed the street to the Adolphus Hotel during the 1960 campaign. As Mike Wallace introduced Dan Rather's report that morning, he struck the note that the national press would follow: "But nowhere is the sense of loss—the sense of shame—greater than in the city of Dallas, Texas, where the president was assassinated."

To some of the reporters who swarmed in from coast to coast, Dallas was part of the South, and therefore a bastion of civil rights abuses. Citing Oswald's bruised face the previous night, they had pressured for proof that officers were not mistreating him—at last badgering police into bringing him out for a midnight showing, where Bill Mercer had remained civil among pushy carpetbaggers.

The worst of them were radio hotshots with portable audiotape recorders. One boasted that his first thought when he'd heard of the assassination was, "Damn it, those rednecks got him!" Proud of his aggression, he later said, "I used these New York City elbows pushing to get into position." Grandstanders with little recorders shoved away print reporters who tried to take notes with pencils that were being shoved into their faces. A shrill little mike-wielder shouted at Captain Fritz, "Sheriff, I demand an answer!" Since the parvenus had taken over our press room desks and dominated the few telephones there, we locals worked around them. Detectives from outside the homicide division were letting some of us into their offices to use phones, and I was thankful that our live television setup communicated with CBS and KRLD.

Our heavy cables were laid down halls and out windows down to controls inside the van, where our cool-headed director, Leigh Webb, ran things. Other cables ran through the chief's office and dangled from his windows to trucks below.

In the crush of reporters I had the advantage of the live camera and lights, along with Benny Molina and our cameraman Gene Pasczalek. Benny, Gene and the heavy equipment afforded a buffer, but when Chief Jesse Curry emerged from Fritz's office into the hall, I was in a free-for-all.

A bouquet of audiotape mikes were competing with my live CBS mike, and other reporters nudged their way in beside me as I asked the chief, "With this man's apparent subversive background, was there any surveillance? Were police aware of his presence in Dallas?"

"We in the police department here did not know he was in Dallas," he said, "I understand the FBI did know that he was in Dallas. We had not been informed of this man." Then a loud chorus of eager guys with recorders drowned me out as I tried to follow up by asking about cooperation between the police, FBI, and Secret Service. One of them asked the chief directions to the county jail. Another braced a notepad against the chief's back as he wrote. I reported, "Police Chief Jesse Curry told us that although the FBI knew of his background and presence in Dallas, the police department was not informed." In Washington, J. Edgar Hoover got the word. Soon the FBI began covering up its knowledge of

Bob Huffaker, barely visible at upper right, asks Chief Jesse Curry, "With this man's apparent subversive background, was there any surveillance? Were police aware of his presence in Dallas?" *Photograph courtesy The Sixth Floor Museum at Dealey Plaza*. Dallas Times Herald *Collection*

Oswald, contradicting Chief Curry's statement and spawning a thousand conspiracy theories.

Introducing my interview with the chief, Walter Cronkite had called me Nelson Benton.

At some point Cronkite spoke of "crank-filled Dallas." We locals regretted that reputation and felt that it was not entirely deserved. But though we had perhaps no more cranks per square mile than many other big cities, ours were hateful, organized, conspicuous, and encouraged by the *Dallas Morning News*. I had suppressed outrage while filming scruffy and swastikaed brownshirts standing at mock attention, and Wes had filmed the Adlai Stevenson indignities a month before. Dallas was beset by some mad right-wingers whose brazen demonstrations had hijacked the city's reputation. By that delirious morning, most of the Dallas media had fielded a bomb threat or two, and police were getting edgy about security, as it became apparent that frenzied reporters were getting out of control. Guards stood watching entrances, but in the Police and Courts Building, lots of people were coming and going to and from other offices.

Nelson and I were sitting shoulder-to-shoulder on the floor, propped against a wall facing the elevators. We watched their doors sliding open and shut, disgorging loads of people. We were talking about the loose security, noticing how people were roaming the halls without any ID check. As another cluster of passengers emerged, I said, "What if somebody stepped out of an elevator and started raking the crowd with a submachine gun?" We watched those sliding doors for a moment, then looked at each other, got up without a word, and moved from the line of fire. From then on, we kept ourselves and our camera crews in the safest positions we could get. We were at the epicenter of a nation rocked by grief and anger, and we began to move with care.

During our vigil at police headquarters that afternoon, Wes Wise was following Oswald's trail through Oak Cliff after a stubby fan of his named Jack Ruby had delayed him at the assassination site. Bill Mercer reported from among the wreaths accumulating there. And high over Dealey Plaza, George Phenix's pilot popped a window open and slipped the plane sideways into a bank as George filmed the line of cars that seemed to reach the horizon, creeping past JFK's death scene, clogging traffic all the way from Deep Ellum.

At police headquarters Oswald's cell was above us on the fifth floor.

To take him from there to Fritz's office, detectives would bring him down the jail elevator, sometimes through the basement jailers' office, then back up to the third floor. The homicide guys tipped me about such movements, so that our basement camera could catch a shot of him as he was taken through the jail office. Nelson would stay with the third-floor mike while I waited for quick glimpses of the silent and defiant Oswald.

After Captain Fritz's morning session with Oswald, I reported from the third-floor hallway, "Oswald is now back upstairs above us in a cell. Homicide officers questioned him for about two hours this morning, and no one knows the outcome, if any. Oswald's young Russian wife and his mother have been inside the homicide office, closeted with officers, but they reportedly have not yet seen Oswald. They left a short while ago—the wife weeping, the mother speechless."

During a long wait while Nelson was keeping the homicide office vigil, I dropped in on Captain Glen King, the chief's assistant for public information. Journalists must continue to check their facts, and I was a firm believer in the reporter's creed, "If your mama says she loves you, check it out." So I sat down across from King with the mimeographed notes that I'd brought along and told him I'd like to double-check the basic facts about Oswald. I ran through them: "Twenty-four years old, ex-Marine, Lee Harvey Oswald—"

"Lee Harold Oswald," he interrupted me.

"Lee *Harold*? Everyone else is reporting Harvey."

"It's Harold."

"Are you absolutely sure?"

"Absolutely."

"Where did you get Harold?"

"Off the arrest record."

On my purple-printed mimeograph sheet headed "Suspect, prime," I marked out Harvey and wrote Harold, then began calling him Lee Harold Oswald. Later I heard Cronkite calling him Lee Henry Oswald, but that didn't take away the sting of having thought that I was the only one who had the middle name right.

As Nelson and I kept reporting throughout that long Saturday, we were concerned with not only facts but also pictures. KRLD's newsman George Phenix was shooting with his big Auricon optical-sound camera, and Nelson and I were trying to get as much video as possible on our live cameras. Rather than breaking into the day's sad and unrelenting news with brief shots of Oswald's passings, we taped them for later broadcast. Today's television makes so big a deal over being live that reporters stand at deserted scenes long after the action is over. We stayed at scenes only when there was a reason, and we left when nothing was to be reported. Instead of wasting time someplace merely to be *live,* we went where things were happening. We reported on the spot if events were urgent, and when they were over, we hurried in with film to develop and stories to write.

Killing a president was not a federal offense in 1963. JFK's murder was covered instead by Texas law, which required that felons, once charged, be jailed by the county where the crime took place. Our best chance to get more pictures of Oswald would be when police transferred him to the custody of Sheriff Bill Decker at the county jail—in a routine now institutionalized as the "perp walk," the public transfer of an accused perpetrator. With the aggressive world press in their faces, Dallas officials were overwhelmed as they tried to satisfy reporters while protecting their prisoner.

On the evening of the assassination, we were already reporting that Oswald, an ex-Marine, had defected to Russia in 1959, married a Russian woman, proclaimed himself a Marxist, and worked for the pro-Castro Fair Play for Cuba Committee. His apparent left-wing background was a paradox in the murder of a liberal president—and the political opposite of ultraconservatives who had disgraced Dallas before. But Oswald was a self-styled Communist ideologue. Enmeshed in this conundrum, the city's oligarchy was horrified that their series of embarrassments had culminated in the worst of possible calamities. They were eager to please the press—too eager, as it turned out.

GIVING THE PRESS A SHOT AT THE PRISONER

Dallas's local media had a history of mutual cooperation with police, sheriff's officers, and firefighters, and even in retrospect I believe that it worked to the community's advantage. Although our lack of adversarial zeal would be inappropriate in today's journalism, we found our first-responders professional, rarely given to brutality, and candid with the press. Knowing that local reporters behaved well at scenes of crime and mishap, they were honest with us, and we were considerate of them. My

Behind the live cameras, KRLD cameraman Jim English at right. *Photograph courtesy The Sixth Floor Museum at Dealey Plaza.* Dallas Times Herald *Collection*

police and highway patrol press cards and windshield pass would get me anywhere within reason. Because we trusted each other in that long-ago window of time, the community was well informed and better protected.

Chief Curry once suspended a cop who tried to block my camera and keep me from filming officers doing a proper job of subduing a fighting drunk at the annual downtown orgy before the Texas-Oklahoma football game. I'd kept the camera rolling, then shown my film in the chief's office. Whatever possessed that misguided patrolman, I considered his butting-in a violation of press freedom. But it was my only such encounter ever, and Curry issued orders forbidding his officers from interfering with journalists doing their job.

Within twenty-four hours of the assassination, hundreds of reporters had converged on Dallas from all over the world. More were coming, and the crowd at police headquarters were a boisterous lot. Chief Curry and Captain Fritz had acquiesced in the bizarre midnight showing of Oswald only to face more demands from reporters, and the two officers were uneasy about the danger of moving such a hated suspect. Fritz wanted to exclude the media and keep the transfer secret. He and Curry discussed moving Oswald at night, but they decided that daylight would help officers see anyone who tried to attack.

In his office Curry finally relented when his boss, City Manager El-
gin Crull, insisted that he allow us access to Oswald to prevent accusations of "Gestapo tactics." The tall and gentlemanly Curry had been
shouted at by reporters who felt that, being a southern city, Dallas must
be policed by fat, club-wielding Bull Connor stereotypes. Among the
hundreds of newsmen who had hit town, many were abandoning civility in a rush to star in covering the story of their careers.

The rest of us played defense. I laid a shoulder into a few aggressors,
but only after they'd shoved me first. Meanwhile, behind closed doors
on the third floor, Captain Fritz accepted Curry's reluctant mandate to
transfer the prisoner in front of the press. Having assented with skep-
ticism, Fritz withdrew somewhat from planning the public transfer that
he'd opposed. He concentrated on questioning Oswald and witnesses
while his detectives went on fitting new scraps of evidence into the sur-
prisingly complete picture they already had assembled.

In the small, dark hours of Sunday morning, Sheriff Bill Decker called
police headquarters to urge that they abort the public transfer and move
Oswald immediately. An anonymous tip had warned of an organized plot
to kill Oswald, and Decker had tried without success to reach Chief
Curry at home. The chief apparently had disabled his home phone after
the *Times-Herald* reporter Darwin Payne awakened him with a call after
midnight. Curry's number was unlisted, but we locals had it.

Shortly before nine o'clock that Sunday morning, Curry rejected
Sheriff Bill Decker's suggestion that they speed the transfer and avoid
the press. Instead, Curry said that he would move Oswald in an armored truck, since a credible report had threatened a coordinated attack to kill the suspect.

I had showed my press credentials that morning to gain admission to
the basement garage, where officers were to bring Oswald past reporters on his way to the vehicle. I also had gotten our camera crews in,
and I showed my press card even to police guards who knew me. Wes
Wise had driven a conspicuously marked KRLD News wagon through
the garage to drop off our film cameraman, George Phenix, before Wes
headed for the county jail to report Oswald's arrival with our live camera there. Although reporters had entered the building without ID
checks, police made us all leave the garage before they posted guards
and searched it. When they were confident that they had cleared the
area, they methodically readmitted us while checking our credentials.

Neither Curry nor Fritz would tell us when they would move Oswald, but the previous night I had said, "Chief, none of us has slept more than a couple of hours since Friday. These guys need some rest. Can you just tell me how early we need to be set up, so that we won't miss the transfer?"

"If you men will be here by ten o'clock in the morning, that will be early enough for you," he said, but I still didn't get much sleep that night. I got up and showered, and before dawn broke I was driving downtown through deserted Sunday morning streets.

4

Epicenter of Grief

BOB HUFFAKER

Nelson Benton, George Phenix, and I were at the Police and Courts Building early, working with the crews to plan our shots of the transfer. Sergeant Patrick T. Dean, in charge of security in the basement that morning, was my best friend in the department. Having worked as a small-town reserve cop, I enjoyed riding with Pat as he oversaw the East Dallas zone, where he supervised fifteen officers in six squads. Pat liked talking to a friend on those long shifts, and when he was off duty, we met for beer and conversation.

Pat came back to work that Sunday after a week of deer hunting in South Texas. When he got to the station before seven o'clock that morning, he'd changed into his uniform in the basement locker room, then gone to the detail room to be briefed by Captain Cecil Talbert. In the briefing, Pat sat with Lieutenant Rio "Sam" Pierce and Jim Putnam, a tall and muscular traffic sergeant who from time to time joined Pat and me after his shift. After Pat had sent out his East Dallas squads, Rio Pierce assigned him to organize basement security, starting with a thorough search of the parking garage. Pat assembled fourteen reserve officers, including the reserve Captain Charles Arnett, and with some men from Pat's own platoon, they set about securing the basement. Shortly after nine o'clock they cleared the parking garage and ramps of newsmen, including Nelson and me, along with George Phenix, who was operating a big sound-on-film camera, and Jim English, who ran our live camera with its big zoom lens. Pat assured us that we could come back into the garage after the search.

Since Nelson was the network guy and I the local, I deferred to him and his CBS producers in the New York studios. They planned to broadcast Oswald's transfer while taping it for rebroadcast. Nelson would sit in the KRLD van outside and narrate the operation while watching it on the monitors. To pick up natural sound, I would be holding the mike with our live basement camera, and I would not speak.

THE ASSASSIN'S ASSASSIN

Across the Trinity in Oak Cliff, fifty-two-year-old Jack Ruby, a police and media groupie who ran a couple of local night clubs, was getting out of bed while his roommate, George Senator, brought up laundry from the apartment building's washroom. Senator, a fifty-year-old former New Yorker who tended bar at the Carousel, Ruby's strip club, noticed that his friend was agitated and abrupt as he made coffee and scrambled eggs. Senator, whom Ruby's sister Eva Grant called "a Jewish housewife," was worried about his roommate.

Ruby had changed his name from Jacob Rubenstein and built his life around his Vegas and Carousel clubs, where he bullied unsteady drunks and sometimes got in fights with his strippers. He was often generous to his employees nonetheless, and he pandered to local media and police—sometimes, I suspect, literally. Since police answered calls to the clubs, plenty of officers, Pat Dean included, knew him from handling minor dustups at his strip joint, the Carousel, and his rock-and-roll club, the Vegas. Some off-duty cops went to those clubs, where Ruby would see that they got special attention, free beer and such. He also bestowed his largesse on reporters and was especially enamored of my buddy Wes Wise, our nightly sportscaster, though none of us at KRLD frequented his clubs.

Ruby had closed the Carousel and Vegas in deference to the slain president's memory, and he had spent Friday night among reporters at police headquarters, even attending the photo-op when police brought Oswald before the press in the assembly room. Later he had brought sandwiches to disc jockeys and newsmen at KLIF, the city's loud and leading Top 40 radio station. Ruby had grown up in Chicago as a minor tough whose short temper had earned him the nickname "Sparky," and he'd cultivated a reputation as a skilled gate-crasher, slipping into ball games and taking friends in with him.

Now Jack Ruby was popping Preludin and Benzedrine, and working himself into a frenzy of righteous anger against JFK's assassin. Ruby had not gone to bed until around six o'clock Saturday morning, and that afternoon tears welled in his eyes as he accosted Wes Wise at Dealey Plaza and displayed his sentiment for Jackie Kennedy and her children, his thin voice cracking into a falsetto.

While we at police headquarters prepared for Oswald's transfer that Sunday morning, Ruby, still in his underwear, watched us on television and succumbed to the nation's grief. The Preludin that he took was an upper, a substitute for amphetamines. It was sold as a diet drug, but it wasn't keeping him from being pudgy, and the speed wasn't helping his mood, especially combined with Benzedrine.

THE DANCER AND THE KILLER

The dance was bumps, grinds, and shimmies. The dancer was Karen Lynn Carlin, who removed her clothes at the Carousel under the name "Little Lynn." She was nineteen, pregnant, and broke. At 10:19 that morning Ruby's phone rang, and she was after him for money again. His generosity was selective. Karen needed twenty-five dollars for groceries and overdue rent; Ruby needed Little Lynn's bare anatomy on his runway. He told her that he was headed downtown anyway. He'd wire the money from the telegraph office. They had talked for two minutes and nineteen seconds.

Jack hung up and George Senator watched as he muttered to himself and paced the floor. Then Ruby shucked his underwear, bathed, dressed, and drove toward the heart of Dallas. Sheba, his favorite dachshund, the one he jokingly called his wife, was on the seat beside him. Under his coat he also took along his little Colt Cobra.

SHOOTING LEE OSWALD

In the police basement, Pat Dean's team was finishing its search operation, and the parking garage was secure, with at least one guard at each door, including the ramp entrances that allowed cars to drive down from Main, then back up onto Commerce. Standing beside our live camera outside the jail office, I watched the armored truck backing into the exit ramp, at Commerce Street. I gave George Phenix a boost, and he hung his film camera's sound mike directly above where Oswald would pass.

Outside in our van, Nelson Benton was watching the monitors. Harry Reasoner was anchoring from New York, and CBS had decided to tape the prisoner's transfer for later broadcast. From the van, Nelson would narrate the transfer as he saw it on our basement camera, then on our outside camera as the armored truck drove away on Commerce Street. Down in the garage, I would point the mike at the action while Nelson spoke from the van. Before Fritz and his men brought Oswald out, I would turn the broadcast over to Nelson. As tension grew, I began narrating the scene for the rolling tapes.

> Strict security precautions have been exercised from the very beginning and have been even increased this morning, as fear arises and grows stronger that someone may attempt to take the life of the man accused of murdering the president of the United States. Inside the basement here at Dallas Police headquarters, guards are stationed at points all across the inside of the basement. All incoming cars throughout the morning have been carefully checked. Even the police vehicles have been searched, inside trunks and inside the rear compartments of paddy wagons that have entered here in the basement. Officers have checked every vehicle coming in, and no one who is not a member of the press and not able to show identification can enter the basement. The basement is empty except for a large gathering of reporters, who are now watching the truck being moved into position. Outside the building a large force of heavily armed police have kept a constant ring around Dallas City Hall, and a comparatively small group of spectators are now gathered across from the basement entrance from which the armored car will depart.
>
> Security precautions have been tightened more and more as the morning has worn on, and according to the people in the jail office, Oswald spent a restful night and got perhaps a good night's sleep. . . . A number of police vehicles are lined up further to our rear here in the basement and are preparing to depart along with the armored vehicle. The car is being backed slowly down the ramp here into the basement. Apparently they're having some difficulty—and apparently the clearance is going to be a little bit high.

People still are wondering exactly when Oswald will come down, and although from yesterday morning it has been known that Oswald would be transferred from the Dallas City Jail to the Dallas County Jail, no one has known exactly when the transfer would take place. It was only known that it would take place when full preliminary questioning had been completed by the office of Dallas Homicide Captain Will Fritz. Far into the night last night reporters kept their vigil here at Dallas City Hall, and only after the announcement came shortly before ten o'clock Central Standard Time was it known that Oswald would be moved today.

Neither I nor Sergeant Pat Dean knew that the armored truck was to be only a decoy. Arguing that the truck was slow and conspicuous, Captain Fritz had persuaded the chief that morning to let him move Oswald in an unmarked car, and they had shifted the transfer route from Elm to Main Street. Pat had updated the route change as he assigned patrolmen to guard intersections all the way to the county jail, but he still thought that he would ride in the armored truck with Oswald. He had placed his men at every garage entrance and elevator, and he had ordered elevator operators not to descend for any reason.

Just down Main Street at the Western Union office, Jack Ruby parked his car and went inside to send Little Lynn her twenty-five dollars. The clerk time-stamped the telegram at 11:17. Ruby turned and walked out, down Main Street toward police headquarters.

In the homicide office, the regional Secret Service chief, Forrest Sorrels, had finished questioning Oswald. Detective Jim Leavelle, wearing a light western-cut coat, put on his matching wide-brimmed hat. He gave Oswald a sweater to put on, then cuffed his prisoner's hands together in front. With a second set of handcuffs, the big forty-four-year-old officer linked his own left hand to Oswald's right. Leavelle was a much larger target than the skinny prisoner he was protecting, and he joked about being in the line of fire, where he might take a round meant for Oswald: "Lee, I hope that if anybody shoots at you, they're as good a shot as you are."

Oswald, stonefaced until then, said, "You're just being melodramatic. There isn't anybody going to shoot at me."

Unknown to most of us waiting for them in the garage, officers were preparing for the new transfer plan. Two unmarked cars would follow the armored truck. The second, bearing Oswald, would turn off after a block and haul ass for Decker's jail, leaving the slow caravan to defend against any attacks. To augment protection for the decoy, the uniformed Lieutenant Rio "Sam" Pierce would lead the armored vehicle with two more men in an unmarked black sedan. But to allow Pierce to get that car out of the basement, detectives had to move the blue unmarked Ford already in place to carry Oswald.

Pat Dean was waiting near the armored truck when Pierce told him, "Pat, get two men to go with me. Now."

Pat sent his fellow sergeants Jim Putnam and Billy Joe Maxey, who got into the unmarked black Ford as Pierce began nosing it through the mass of cops and reporters. All available officers had been ordered to the garage, where tension was rising as some seventy-five cops and fifty newsmen waited for Oswald to emerge from the jail office. The armored truck was blocking the exit ramp, so big Jim Putnam got out of his seat beside Rio Pierce and moved newsmen aside so that the lieutenant could drive up the down ramp and circle the block to lead the decoy truck.

In front of my position near the bottom of the ramp, Putnam climbed back in as Pierce hit the accelerator. As they squealed past me up the exit ramp, I held the mike and flattened against the railing. Just off the ramp Jim English bent into the monitor of our live camera, his big zoom lens positioned to my left through the railing's horizontal bars. George Phenix stood ready with his film camera on my right.

As Pierce's car barreled up the ramp with red lights flashing through its grille, Roy Vaughn, the patrolman Pat had assigned to guard the entrance, stepped out to the curb to make way and look out for oncoming traffic. As Rio Pierce made an illegal left turn onto Main Street, Jack Ruby walked into the entrance and down the ramp toward me. Vaughn had not seen him.

George Phenix and I did not know Jack Ruby, and we paid him no notice as he sidled in beside George, who was balancing his big sound-on-film camera on a unipod at my right. There at the foot of the ramp, reporters were nudging me as I tried to keep them from blocking Jim English's live camera at my left. George and I were intent on Oswald's imminent arrival, and we paid no attention to Ruby as he walked down and blended with us. Even if Putnam or Pierce had seen him on their way out, they might not have thought much of it. Ruby was a hanger-on, a fixture at the cop shop. His Chicago gate-crashing skills had gotten him in unseen.

As Ruby seethed at George's elbow, Fritz's detective C. W. Brown was repositioning the light-blue car that he'd moved to let Pierce out. He was trying to bring it near the jail office door and shorten the distance Oswald would walk in the open. Things were moving fast, and Fritz got the go-ahead to bring Oswald out before Brown had the blue Ford in place. Brown was backing the unmarked sedan in among us just as the homicide captain emerged ahead of Oswald at 11:21. The young assassin came out glaring at the crowd, Detective L. C. Graves on his left and big Jim Leavelle cuffed to his right wrist. As Brown backed the Ford toward us in a hurry, he sounded its horn, and just as I turned toward the oncoming sedan, Jack Ruby lunged from beside George Phenix with his little revolver and fired a single round point-blank into Oswald's left lower chest.

I spun toward the sound of the gunshot and saw Oswald grimace and crumple into a pileup of men who were subduing and disarming Ruby. Pat Dean was halfway up the ramp near the armored truck when he saw a figure dart toward Oswald. Pat ran up and over the hood of Brown's car to join the scramble. Jim Leavelle, pulled partway down by handcuffs to the falling victim, seized Ruby's left shoulder with his free right hand while L.C. Graves, gripping the revolver's cylinder hard to stop the hammer, pushed Ruby's arm down and wrenched away the gun. Within seconds they and other officers had dragged Ruby and Oswald into the jail office and out of my sight.

There was such a tangle of cops atop the gunman and victim that I couldn't recognize anyone in the fight. Several officers drew pistols. Dick Swain, a burly detective, was shielding the melee with his wide body and shouting to any and all comers, "I'll knock you on your ass!" Police had guns out, and I was uneasy as I aimed the CBS mike at them.

Fort Worth's WBAP-TV was feeding NBC correspondent Tom Pettit's broadcasts from their engine-challenged van, which a wrecker had deposited at the curb. Pettit's guys in New York had switched to him when he said, "Let me have it. I want it." Their NBC cameraman had to take a wide establishing shot, then rack his lens turret on the air for a tight shot of the shooting, while our Jim English had the optical advantage with our camera's giant zoom lens. Jim zoomed out and framed the struggle as detectives dragged both Ruby and Oswald toward the jail office. Jim had a headset, but I had no way to communicate with anyone. Bob Hankal, our floor director, also with a headset, had been stationed left of the lens, but I lost sight of him as the brawl tossed me hard to the right.

Seconds after the shot, I knew that from up in our vans, Nelson couldn't possibly figure things out on the monitors. I couldn't distinguish one torso from another in the fracas as I fought to keep my footing. Twice I said, "Oswald has been shot." Then to avoid covering up anything Nelson might be saying, I stopped talking, hoping that Nelson had heard me. He hadn't.

With tapes rolling in both Dallas and New York, Nelson had begun his broadcast a split second after Ruby pulled the trigger. Not having heard the gunshot, he said, "This is the basement of Dallas City Hall, and there's a scuffle down there." As Nelson continued to talk, I was saying, "Oswald has been shot. Oswald has been shot." I was trying to stay out of our camera's field of view, and I fell silent so that I wouldn't conflict with Nelson's reporting. Neither of us could hear the other, and Nelson was reaching for words as he found it impossible to see what was happening on the black-and-white monitors. He began trying to reach me, but I couldn't hear as he said on the air, "We're going to try to bring in Bob Huffaker of KRLD. Bob, can you hear us down there? Can you give us an account of what happened?"

I couldn't hear anything except the din in the basement. Jim English was glued to his camera and unable to tell me anything, and Bob Hankal had disappeared, headset and all. People were stepping on my mike cord and my feet, pushing and elbowing, wrestling and shouting.

I had stayed out of Jim's camera angles, but without hearing Nelson I at last faced the big zoom lens and started to report. I repeated that Oswald had been shot, and since I had not been able to see the gunman, I continued, "We saw no one fire the shot, only a blast from some bullet here in the basement of Dallas Police headquarters. Oswald fell to the concrete in front of our eyes and immediately was covered by police officers who took him quickly, immediately, instantly from our sight. Police have ringed the inside, and no one is allowed to leave. Everyone is being held in place, and police officers are not even allowing anyone to move. And no one is—" I faltered as I buckled under the weight of reporters crowding in upon me. They were stepping on my mike cord, and I held tight as it pulled me down. I regained my footing at a low crouch and

Moments after Oswald was shot, Bob Huffaker reports for CBS while Tom Pettit (left) feeds NBC. *Photograph courtesy The Sixth Floor Museum at Dealey Plaza. KRLD-TV/KDFW Collection*

thrust upward as hard as I could, shoving men off my shoulders on the way up through the brawl.

"I hope I killed the son of a bitch," Ruby was saying under the pileup of officers in the jail office. Pat Dean, having jumped over the car in the basement, had helped drag the disarmed Ruby and the unconscious Oswald into the office. He peered into the pile of men on top of Ruby and asked, "Who in the hell is it?"

"I'm Jack Ruby," the groupie said from the floor. "You all know me!"

"Jack, Jack," Pat shook his head, "you son of a bitch!"

In the garage I held out my mike as Francois Pelou, an excited French reporter, said, "I saw the flash on the black sweater. I saw the man! He was a stocky guy, well dressed. He had a hat and coat. I thought he was a Secret Service agent!" I reported his mistaken impression on the air, and on CBS Harry Reasoner speculated whether a Secret Service agent might have taken vengeance for the president's murder.

As I went on talking in the basement, Nelson's voice sometimes was covering up my audio while we were live on the network. I was saying, "We can hear sirens outside, and an ambulance is—moving down now

As Oswald is loaded into the ambulance, Bob Huffaker reports, "He is ashen and unconscious at this time." *Photograph courtesy The Sixth Floor Museum at Dealey Plaza. KRLD-TV/KDFW Collection*

into the basement. And Oswald will be moved now. The ambulance is being pulled up in front of us here." The ambulance had come down the entrance ramp and stopped with its tailgate directly in front of Jim English's camera. Pat Dean came out of the jail office and locked arms with all available officers to cordon off the ramp as attendants placed Oswald on the gurney and prepared to bring him out.

I was trying to keep our live camera shot clear, and Pat Dean's butt was directly in front of the lens. On national television, I reached up and patted the sergeant on the side: "Pat, can you move? Pat, move just a little to your left." He held tight within the circle of officers, but he looked down at me and edged over enough for our camera to show Oswald being rolled out and loaded into the ambulance. "Here comes Oswald," I reported. "He is ashen and unconscious at this time. Now he's being moved in. He's not moving."

As a reserve cop in Bryan I'd sometimes carried a Colt Cobra like Ruby's, and having recognized the pop of that small pistol, I didn't expect that Oswald's wound would be mortal. I'd investigated a guy who'd taken a few rounds from a .38, then beaten the daylights out of the shooter.

There were plenty of such tales, but I didn't realize that Ruby's bullet had taken a particularly deadly path.

Oswald was bleeding internally from massive damage, and seconds ebbed as the armored truck's driver moved it from the exit ramp to let the ambulance out. Nelson took over our narration as the ambulance sped up the ramp and off to Parkland with Oswald. They were headed to the trauma center where the president had been pronounced dead two days earlier.

From CBS in New York, Harry Reasoner began, "We have just watched a fantastic scene in Dallas." Reasoner wasn't a fellow to throw the word "fantastic" around.

As soon as police had both Oswald and Ruby out of the jail office— Ruby straight up the elevator to the jail—they allowed reporters to move again. I described Oswald's departure and summarized his shooting on CBS while Tom Pettit continued for NBC.

To follow the action, most of the newsmen left the parking garage and went inside where information was. When they thinned out, Tom and I were left on the ramp in front of the two network cameras. Those big cameras' cables were laid in place, and since disconnecting and relocating them was out of the question, Tom and I were stuck in the garage with no source of facts. Neither of us had gotten a look at Ruby, and I was trying to find out as much as possible about who had shot Oswald.

THE SERGEANT AND I

After the ambulance ascended the ramp and screamed off down Commerce Street, I turned to Pat Dean and began asking questions. He and I both knew that whatever we said might prejudice a case against the shooter. Pat knew Ruby, but he couldn't release his name. Knowing nothing of the shooter, I tried to get information without pressing Pat too far. I made room for Tom Pettit, who came in on the interview while I asked Pat enough to find that the assailant was a local businessman. I said, "Pat, do you know this subject?"

"Yes," he said.

Pat was in an awkward position, a policeman thrust onto national television in the vortex of a national tragedy, and I was trying to protect him while trying to get facts. "Pat, do you know this subject, and did you recognize him?"

In the confusion after Ruby shot Oswald, Bob Huffaker asks Sgt. Patrick Dean, "Pat, do you know this subject?" *Photograph courtesy The Sixth Floor Museum at Dealey Plaza. KRLD-TV/KDFW Collection*

"I do know the man. I'd have known him on sight. If I'd seen him or noticed him, I would have ejected him."

Tom and I were trying to get the story straight while reporters who knew even less than we did kept breaking into the interview to ask how many shots had been fired. After I'd heard that question several times, I started answering it myself. After the interview, Pettit said, "I really appreciate what you just did."

"You, too, Tom. You're one of the good guys." We'd just broadcast television's first murder. I had missed Oswald's middle name, and Nelson had called the place the Houston County Jail once, but I had managed to stand up and hang onto the mike.

When Pat left the garage, anticipating more questions from the press, he headed for Fritz's office to find out when he could release Ruby's name if reporters asked again. But on the third floor, Pat encountered Chief Curry, along with sixty-three-year-old Forrest Sorrels, head of the Dallas Secret Service office for decades. Curry took out his own key ring and handed it to Pat. "Sergeant Dean, please use the third-floor jail elevator door and take Mr. Sorrels up to see Ruby."

Up on the fifth floor Pat stood in the jail with the veteran agent while Ruby, stripped to his underwear, poured out his strange rationale for killing Oswald: a torrent of maudlin sentimentality and self-righteous pity for the slain president's widow and children. Ruby began by asking whether Sorrels was there to interview him for the press. Even though Ruby claimed that he believed in due process of law, he said that he had wanted to spare Jackie and patrolman J. D. Tippit's family the agony of a long trial. In a hurry to report his findings to Washington, Sorrels listened for about ten minutes before he said, "Okay, thank you" and turned to leave.

Pat had gone to great lengths to secure the basement garage. Now he was trying to find out what had gone wrong. He didn't know that Ruby had been at Oswald's Friday night showing in the assembly room, and he said, "Ruby, I want to ask you some questions myself."

"All right."

"How did you get into the basement?"

"I walked in the Main Street ramp. I've just been to the Western Union to send a money order to Fort Worth. I walked from Western Union to the ramp and saw Sam Pierce drive out." Ruby was using Rio Pierce's nickname. "At the time the car drove out is when I walked in."

"How long had you been in the basement when Oswald came into your view?"

"I just walked in. I just walked to the bottom of the ramp when he came out."

The sergeant and the Secret Service supervisor left Ruby sitting in his shorts, fat and disheveled. Pat rode down with Sorrels, retrieved his pistol from the jail office, and took Jesse Curry's keys back to the chief's office. Then he headed for Parkland.

Tom Pettit's NBC crew unhooked their camera and dollied it into the basement lobby, and I went on interviewing reserve Captain Charles Arnett, who knew little and could say less. The NBC crew moved inside, leaving me alone in the garage interviewing any cop I could buttonhole. At last there was nothing left to be learned, so I wrapped things up from there. The Commerce Street guards finally allowed Nelson through. He walked down the ramp and said, "Oh, Bob? When's the next shooting scheduled?"

He stayed below while I sprinted up three flights to our third-floor camera and waited for the next release of information. At Parkland, doctors Tom Shires, Robert McClelland, and Malcolm Perry fought against the shock of massive blood loss that was killing Oswald. Their trauma team cut straight down into big veins and started fluids into his bloodstream nineteen minutes after the slug had clipped both the aorta and the inferior vena cava, the two big vessels in and out of the heart. That combination of circulatory wounds is almost certainly fatal, and an overwhelming volume of blood had hemorrhaged into Oswald's abdominal cavity. The doctors were transfusing sixteen pints of blood into his system as they opened his chest, clamped the leaking vessels, massaged his failing heart, and tried electric defibrillation to no avail.

Ruby's bullet had penetrated Oswald's left lower chest and passed through every major organ and vessel in the abdominal cavity. He'd lost too much blood too fast, and an hour and forty-six minutes after Ruby shot him, they pronounced him dead. They retrieved the lethal bullet from just beneath the skin where it had lodged after traversing Oswald's body. Detective Jim Leavelle, who had climbed into the ambulance and never left his prisoner's side, took the bullet as evidence and slipped it into his pocket.

Doctors Malcolm Perry and Robert McClelland had performed the tracheotomy on the president two days before, and their coats were stained with blood of his assassin, which also soaked the coat of Tom Shires, the surgical chief, who had flown back from a Galveston conference and taken over care of Governor Connally.

Sergeant Pat Dean, worried over the failure of his basement security operation, had gone to Parkland out of a lingering sense of responsibility for Oswald's safety. Having done his best to stop Ruby, he wanted to stay on the job. Pat had not expected the prisoner to die, and he waited outside the trauma room and talked to Oswald's mother and wife, who had arrived by the time the strange son and estranged husband was pronounced dead at 1:07. After Pat escorted the two women in to view his body, there was nothing left to protect.

Pat came back to headquarters and told his superior officer, Lieutenant Pierce, that Ruby had gotten past Patrolman Roy Vaughn at the Main Street garage entrance. Against all evidence to the contrary, Vaughn later swore that it couldn't have happened. But both the cops and the feds concluded that it had, and Pierce reduced Vaughn's efficiency rating on his next report.

It was 1:30 when Chief Jesse Curry appeared before us in the assembly room and announced, "My statement will be very brief. Oswald expired at 1:07 P.M."

I was as surprised as the rest of the press corps for a second. Then a reporter behind me said, "He died?"

"He died. At 1:07 P.M. We have arrested the man. The man will be charged with murder."

"Who is it?"

"The suspect's name is Jack Rubenstein, I believe," the chief said, glancing at Captain Glen King, who nodded confirmation. "He goes by the name of Jack Ruby. That's all I have to say."

Curry turned and walked out of the assembly room, ignoring questions that reporters shouted at him. They ran for telephones, and I went and

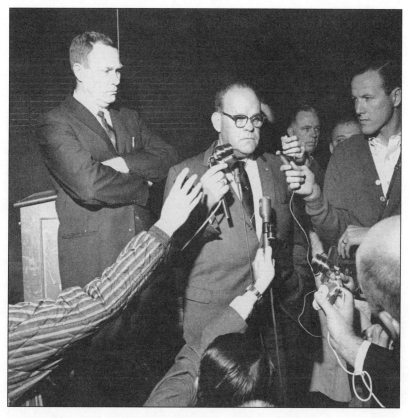

Chief Jesse Curry announces Oswald's death. Capt. Glen King watches with arms folded. *Photograph courtesy The Sixth Floor Museum at Dealey Plaza. Tom Dillard Collection, the* Dallas Morning News

fed KRLD radio while Harry Reasoner was reporting Oswald's death on CBS television. He expressed surprise that the Dallas cops couldn't protect their own prisoner, but he didn't mention the mob of reporters they had been trying to satisfy.

We wanted to know Ruby's motive, which had been clear to police from the moment they subdued him: Jack Ruby was a self-styled tough guy who wanted to be somebody. But Harry Reasoner later summed him up as "a little leftover character."

JACK'S SISTER

Ruby had called his sister, Eva Grant, just before one o'clock that morning. He was acting even stranger than usual, rambling on about attending Officer Tippit's funeral, and Eva was not feeling well that night. She didn't want to talk much, and when Jack kept asking whether she was okay, she convinced him that she wasn't that sick, just not ready to discuss going to the policeman's funeral. The evening before, when Ruby stopped off at her place venting anger at Oswald and sorrow at JFK's murder, Eva had told him, "Don't worry. Some lousy Communist will get him before anyone else does." But her brother got to him first.

That Sunday, still feeling rotten, Eva Grant had passed the morning with her television set on, but she had the sound turned down and was paying little notice to its continuing story of national tragedy. She had first learned of the Oswald shooting as the networks replayed tapes of Tom Pettit and me. Tom had initially called the shooter "Jack Loby," and Eva didn't yet know that the man was her brother.

A musician from the Vegas Club had dropped in for a chat, when a friend of Eva's called: "Eva, I don't want to be the one who tells you this. Do you know who shot Oswald?"

"No."

"Jack shot Oswald."

Eva Grant had seen our reruns of the catastrophe in the basement, and she was aware of the melee but not the facts. When she heard that her brother was the shooter, at first she became frantic, fearing that Jack might have been killed too. Then when her caller made Eva understand that her delusional brother was alive in jail, she began wondering how she could help him. Eva was a tough old bird, but having watched our coverage for the past two days, she feared the media-driven chaos at police headquarters.

Eva Grant wanted someone she could trust to get her through the confusion she was watching on the screen as reporters jammed police hallways, and she called her favorite television weatherman. Jim Underwood answered the phone in our newsroom, and Eva asked him to get her past reporters to see her brother. Eva watched Jim's Channel 4 weathercasts every evening, and she trusted this articulate and wise gentleman. Underwood's wavy hair was gray-streaked, his familiar voice friendly. He was as trustworthy as he looked on television, and he had the air of a statesman.

Like the rest of us, Jim was a reporter. Riding in the motorcade a few cars behind the president's with *Times-Herald* photographer Bob Jackson, Jim had heard Oswald's three shots from directly above. Bob had looked up and seen the rifle. Jim, who had ducked heavy rifle fire in combat, had vaulted out and run toward the greatest danger, where people were throwing themselves on the ground as bullets slammed into the president.

When Eva Grant called Jim, he promised to pick her up at her Oak Lawn apartment, and when Will Fritz's detectives called to offer her a ride to their office, she told them that she already had one. She wanted Jim to be her escort.

Outside the homicide office, I was surprised to see Jim leading her through the mob of reporters in the hallway. "This is Eva Grant," he said, "Ruby's sister. She wants me to get her in to see Fritz." Eva, accompanied by her friend Pauline Hall, who had ridden along to the police station, was barely visible behind a white veil. Jim and I looked at each other with a little shrug at the strangeness of our situation. As I held the CBS mike, tapes were rolling in both New York and Dallas, and I knew that either control center might put us on live at the flip of a switch.

"Okay, Jim," I said as I stepped aside for him and his charge. As it turned out, Eva didn't want to speak at all, and she was depending on Jim to be her spokesman. When Jim went into the homicide office, a couple of obnoxious guys with audiotape recorders took it ill that he'd gone where they weren't admitted, and they began a strident and unrelenting protest: "If he has a right to be in there, we have a right to be in there! If he has a right to be in there, we have a right to be in there!" I

KRLD Assistant News Director Jim Underwood points the way to veiled Eva Grant and her friend Pauline Hall approaching the homicide office. *Photograph courtesy The Sixth Floor Museum at Dealey Plaza.* Dallas Times Herald *Collection*

wondered what more they expected from police who had cooperated so fully that they'd lost the prisoner of the century.

They clamored so that Jim emerged from Fritz's office and said, "Listen, fellows, I'm not going upstairs into the jail. I'm just trying to make arrangements for this woman to see her brother."

I had the live mike in Jim's face when one of the shrill guys thrust his recorder's little mike in alongside mine and asked, "What is her address?"

I'd seen enough shooting. Bearing in mind the danger of publicizing addresses in that atmosphere of insanity and violence, I said, "Jim, would you please not answer that question just yet?"

Beside me, I heard the guy taping in a feverish rush, "Ladies and gentlemen, KRLD newsman Bob Huffaker has just prevented KRLD newsman Jim Underwood from answering my question!"

I lowered the mike and covered it with my hand, then turned to the fellow and said, "Look, if you want to get someone else killed, just don't do it through my mike."

In secret the next day, Fritz's detectives hustled Ruby out of his cell, down the jail elevator, and through the door where Oswald had taken his last steps. They stuffed the chubby prisoner into the back seat of an unmarked car. Two officers sat against him to shield against attack, and behind a motorcycle escort they sped to the county jail with a backup car bearing four more officers—taking the same route they'd planned for the assassin he'd killed. At the jail's loading dock, they emerged wielding shotguns and warning a few surprised reporters to keep their distance as they jogged Ruby inside to what would become his last place of residence.

FILM OF THE PRESIDENT'S DEATH

While Jack Ruby had been intervening to confuse an already complicated tale, Dan Rather, the CBS Southwest Bureau chief, had been negotiating to buy the 8 mm color movie film that Abraham Zapruder had taken of the fatal bullet striking JFK. The Time-Life corporation outbid him and bought the only film that had captured the terrible sight. We were not allowed to show the film, so each of the three networks could only describe what it revealed. Dan brought a 16 mm print of the film to our newsroom a few days after the assassination, and he and I took it into the projection room. Dan had to view it and feed a report about it to Walter Cronkite's evening news. I ran the soundless film over and over again for the better part of an hour while Dan took notes.

We timed the bullets' impacts and noted how the president's head and body reacted to the two shots that hit their mark. We did not know then that the first of the three shots had ricocheted off an oak limb and hit a Main Street curb. When the second one strikes Kennedy in the upper back, a road sign obscures the president in Abraham Zapruder's frame, which shows Governor Connally react to the shot from the back. The film shows JFK grasping at his throat when he reappears from behind the sign. As Kennedy holds both arms upward toward his throat where the bullet had emerged, Governor Connally, having glanced over his right shoulder at the sound of the first shot, which had missed, slumps after being hit by the same slug that wounds the president. Then the third and final shot hits the back of Kennedy's head, which is tilted forward when the bullet blasts away a massive section of right rear skull and brain. The bullet's plowing through the right posterior brain causes the president's head to snap to the left and roll violently back toward his horrified wife.

As I ran the now-famous film time after time, Dan and I talked about what its fuzzy sequence revealed. Dan was well acquainted with firearms, and I'd been an expert army rifleman. We agreed that the film showed reactions to at least two hits from behind, consistent with ballistics evidence of shots fired from the sixth floor. I'd worn a lumbar back brace like the president's, and right or wrong, I speculated that the corsetlike device might have helped to hold JFK up and account for the backward movement of his head and upper body when the final shot had struck.

Dan went to a typewriter, then into our television studio, where he reported our conclusions for CBS. Like the rest of us, he read directly from the copy he wrote, since TelePrompTers were still in their early stages of development. Dan, who had begun his career at KSAM in Huntsville while he was attending Sam Houston State, and while I was at KORA in Bryan thirty miles away, was a careful and wise journalist. Years later some assassination buffs labeled him a conspirator for distorting what Zapruder's film showed as he reported it that evening. That would make both of us part of the conspiracy.

BARKER VS. RATHER

A few days later, Dan and Eddie Barker got into a dispute over whether students at University Park Elementary School had cheered upon hearing of the president's death. Dan had a tip that such a reaction had happened, and Eddie, sensitive about Dallas' reputation, doubted its accuracy. Eddie and Jane Barker had five children, and three of them attended that school, whose officials had assured Eddie that their students had been shocked at the news and that none had cheered, with the possible exception of a few uncomprehending kids who'd just learned that school was out.

Eddie's temper was legendary. He called himself our "Old Captain," and he ran a tight ship. If something set him off, he would emerge purple-faced from his office and kick the nearest trash can spiraling across the newsroom floor, scattering fanfolds of discarded teletype copy on an eccentric trajectory. His instincts were on target even when his outbursts weren't, and he usually aimed his spectacular explosions at some junior staffer who'd messed up.

Eddie Barker had broken into radio as a *wunderkind,* announcing high school football between his sophomore and junior years in San Antonio's

Harlandale High School. He'd been only twenty when he began sixteen years of broadcasting Southwest Conference network games, and he had joined KRLD on December 12, 1949—Channel 4's first day on the air. Eddie had grown up as one of the top names in Texas broadcasting— quick, talented, and skilled in news and weather as well as sports play-by-play. He had designed and built KRLD News, adopting the format and organization of a network operation while Fort Worth's Channel 5 was still running its "Texas News" as voice over film, like newsreels at the movies. He had earned his reputation, and the Old Captain dominated the bridge.

Eddie had told Dan Rather that the story of the school children's cheering was false. When Dan fed it to CBS anyway, Eddie was furious.

He descended on Dan and his CBS crew in a rage, and like driving money-changers from the temple, the Old Captain threw them out of his newsroom, one and all. "Out," he ordered as he pointed the way. They scrambled to collect film cameras, portable lights and audio gear, then loaded up like hurricane refugees and hauled it all to a hotel.

The stunned and banished CBS crew exceeded thirty people, and their forced exodus was a rare moment in broadcast history. Networks expected cooperation from their local stations, and rumblings ensued about our losing our CBS affiliation. KRLD's management backed Eddie, and it took a few days of diplomacy to get Dan and his people back into the newsroom. When at last Nelson Benton walked back in, he looked at me for a second and raised his eyebrows, but we shrugged and left any comment to our respective bosses.

WITNESSES AFTER THE FACT

Reporters who had been near the assassination and its aftermath soon found their positions reversed. We'd been interviewing law officers, and now they began interviewing us as they investigated the deaths of Kennedy, Tippit, and Oswald. FBI, Secret Service, Texas Rangers, CIA, Army Intelligence, Dallas Police Criminal Investigation Division, and other investigators sought us out. George Phenix and I were witnesses to Ruby's murder of Oswald. Wes Wise, whom Ruby accosted the day before he shot Oswald, became a witness for both sides in the coming trial. Jim Underwood and Bob Jackson, who won a Pulitzer for his *Times-Herald* photo of the Oswald shooting, were in the motorcade when the sniper fired from above them at his sixth-floor perch, and they became Warren Commission witnesses along with George and me.

At the FBI offices in the Dallas Federal Building four days after Ruby shot Oswald, I met with agents Ed Hardin and Ralph Rawlings. They were not wasting time in getting witness accounts of the shooting, and their questions centered upon precise details: where I was standing, where my eyes were focused, what I saw and heard before and after the sound of that little pistol. Hardin and Rawlings were careful to ask what security measures I'd seen police taking that Sunday. I told them that no one had asked for identification when I'd entered the Main Street door of the Dallas Police and Courts Building before eight o'clock that morning. "But when I got off the elevator on the third floor," I said, "officers made me show my press card, even though some of them knew me by sight."

I told the agents that the thoroughness of Sergeant Patrick Dean's basement security had impressed me. Pat and Sergeant Jim Putnam had cleared us from the basement garage before their search, and their men checked our credentials as they readmitted my crew and me. I had even seen Putnam search a police van that came down the ramp. Pat's search team had opened the trunks and hoods of cars already parked there. Agents Hardin and Rawlings wrote in their report, "Huffaker stated that the quick movement of RUBY toward OSWALD would not have attracted his attention, inasmuch as the seventy-five or more newsmen in the area were constantly jostling for position, and it was not uncommon for one of them to jostle against another or to move quickly to a more advantageous site." No kidding. Some visiting reporters displayed neither dignity nor manners. I wasn't proud to be among them.

The FBI seemed determined to get this investigation right, and two days later, two more agents paid me a Saturday visit at my apartment off "Deep Ellum," the east end of Elm Street. A week before, the president had died at Dealey Plaza on Elm's west end. Nat Pinkston and Harlan Brown doffed their snap-brims and settled on my couch. I poured coffee, and they got down to business.

Like Hardin and Rawlings, Pinkston and Brown were cast from similar molds—clean-cut fellows in modest ties and dark suit coats that hung loose for a quick draw. They were likable and polite, with no time to waste. They wanted to know the names of everyone I'd recognized in the basement garage. My visitors asked me all the precise questions that the other agents had raised in their offices, and they didn't mind the chicory in my coffee.

Pinkston and Brown wrote of me, "He observed guards at both ends of the drive-through ramp and he saw officers searching the cars in the parking area in the basement prior to the time OSWALD was brought out of the jail." While these agents were assembling facts, a few others were covering the FBI's ass by hiding what they'd known of Oswald.

When Pinkston and Brown filed their report on the following Monday, I was many miles south at Fort Hood, beginning two weeks' reserve duty in the Army. At Eddie's request I had postponed my annual active duty so long that I served that year's so-called summer camp in the dead of winter. Fort Hood was even bleaker than usual in the bitter cold when I reported in to some outfit that had no use for me at all. The overcast skies and desolate landscape were uniformly gray, and the north wind whipped through as I checked into drafty World War II bachelor officers' quarters. To get the heat turned on, I had to call the post engineer and impersonate a colonel. But after the past two weeks' nightmare, I was glad to escape Dallas and be a soldier again for a while.

But even back in uniform I couldn't elude the assassination's unrelenting investigation. On Wednesday of my first week on duty there, the Dallas cops came after me. While the feds were chasing down other witnesses, the police Special Services Bureau was on the case and moving fast. Two SSB lieutenants drove the 150 miles south to the sprawling installation to question me. Jack Revill and F. I. Cornwall pulled up to my BOQ in a black unmarked Ford and came to my rooms for essentially the same discussion that I'd had with the two FBI teams. We three lieutenants sat around a table in the plywood building and went over details of where I was standing and what I had observed in the police garage that Sunday morning ten days before. Jack Revill was the principal investigator, and he asked most of the questions. "The only KRLD people down there with me were George Phenix with the film camera, Jim English behind the live camera, and Bob Hankal, our floor director," I told them.

"Do you recall where they were standing in relation to your position?" Revill asked.

"Phenix was just to my right, Jim had his zoom lens stuck between the rails of the ramp to my left, and Bob was just to the left of Jim's camera."

After an hour or so, Revill and Cornwall decided that their officer

W. J. Harrison had been just to my right, somewhere near Phenix's position. I had not told them so, since I didn't know where detective Blackie Harrison had been, but they had already assembled enough witness accounts to draw that conclusion. They were reconstructing the scene of the shooting, and I wished that I could have helped them more after their long drive.

"Did you know Jack Ruby?"

"No, I knew several of the policemen down there, and I'd talked to Tom Pettit, but Phenix, English and Hankal were the only others I knew."

Revill and Cornwall asked whether the FBI had interviewed me yet. They were sharing witnesses with the feds, although they were keeping their investigation independent. I told them about my interviews with Hardin and Rawlings and Pinkston and Brown. Then, leaving me at windswept Fort Hood, the SSB lieutenants headed to Austin, then Houston, questioning other witnesses who had been in the basement.

In Washington the next day, December 5, the newly established Warren Commission met for the first time. Soon the President's Commission on the Assassination of President John F. Kennedy would be sending deposition attorneys to Dallas, and I was going to hear from them, too.

When I got back to Dallas, Eddie proclaimed me the KRLD News expert on our videotapes of the Oswald shooting, and every few days I stood with Secret Service, FBI, Warren Commission, and police investigators as our engineers racked up two-inch-wide videotapes on the big reel-to-reel machine that stood on the film-room floor. While they timed the sequence of events with stopwatches, I pointed out movements. Again and again, we marked time spans like the fifty-five seconds between Rio Pierce's driving up the ramp and Ruby's pulling the trigger. Watching myself misstate Oswald's middle name on scores of replays reinforced my sense of humility, and this video déjà vu was a bizarre experience.

THE ASSASSIN'S MOTHER

Lee Oswald had been dead and buried for a few days when Eddie assigned me to interview his mother. Having seen Marguerite Oswald's son murdered before my eyes, I dreaded intruding upon this mother's grief. But she turned out to be so aggressive and full of tough rhetoric that I found myself feeling little sympathy.

On the telephone, I asked Mrs. Oswald what she thought might have happened if her son had been brought to trial. "Well," she evaded the question, "of what might have happened, I think what is happening now all over this country, that people are wondering about just exactly what happened. I receive letters continuously. The picture has changed in this old house in the last ten days. We have letters from very prominent people—business people, lawyers, ministers and so on, where in the beginning I was getting cards from mothers . . . sympathy and religious cards. Now that the shock—this is my own idea—now that the shock of the president's death has, ah, been satisfied, then they started to realize about a boy who was handcuffed and how he was shot down even though he said he was innocent and wasn't given a chance in our courts of law, which is our American way of life."

"What is your opinion about the innocence or guilt of your son?"

"Well, I know that my son is innocent."

"You do not feel that the charges against him were justified then?"

"Well, it's not that I do not feel. I know that they were not justified, because I know that my son is innocent."

"And on what facts do you base this knowledge?"

"On the same facts that are being produced now by very prominent people. It would take a lot to go into them. . . . And I don't believe that Lee did it, because I think, had he done something like that, he would have been more than glad to say that he did it. He would have did it for a cause, and he would have wanted to discuss it! And so that's why I happen to know that he didn't do it."

"What do you have to say about the evidence which Dallas County officers and city officers have made public in regard to the case which was being compiled against your son. That is, the handprint on the gun—"

"Well as a layman," she interrupted, "I can almost—it's just ridiculous. I'm not an attorney, I'm not a anybody but just a layman, but I'm stupid enough to know—not to know—that just in a few hours time this evidence could be compiled against anyone, whether it's my son or not. I happen to watch television, and I read a lot, and I happen to know of some of American way of life. And I know that these bullets would have to be tested and all kind of tests, and, well, it just would've been impossible in a few hours' time to point to anybody, whether it's Lee or anybody else, as being the guilty one, because they just wouldn't have had time to do anything about that. It's all circumstantial evidence."

"Well now, you are aware that the bullets were tested and were sent off for this purpose, and the results show that they did come from the gun which they have identified as Lee's."

"Yes, I'm aware of that through the newspapers, but that doesn't mean that Lee shot the gun."

"They also, of course, placed him in the room at the time of the shooting, and also identified his handprint on the stock of the gun."

"Well, I have different information. . . . Some of the bigger men, big men in this country, are wondering about things like that. . . . This gun was in the Paine garage and never in Lee's room in Dallas."

The day before he used his rifle to kill the president, her son had retrieved the weapon from the garage of Ruth Paine in suburban Irving, where Marina, his estranged wife, lived with their two young children. The morning of the assassination, he smuggled it into the School Book Depository in a long bag he'd made from brown paper. He rode to Irving, then back to Dallas, with a coworker who lived near Ruth Paine, and who asked him that morning what was in the bag. "Curtain rods," he'd answered, and they hadn't talked much on that ride to work. Police found the bag and rifle on the sixth floor. All forensic analyses linked both to Oswald.

Later that day when Ruth Paine told Marina that the president had been shot from the building where Lee worked, the pretty Russian mother feared the worst. "My heart dropped," she said later. "I then went to the garage to see whether the rifle was there, and I saw that the blanket was still there and I said, 'Thank God!'" Oswald had kept the weapon rolled in a blanket, which he had re-rolled after taking the rifle. When Marina showed the blanket to officers who arrived, her heart sank again. When they lifted it, the roll hung empty in their hands.

Marguerite Oswald continued her conversation with me in rapid-fire argument, suggesting that someone might have offered to take Lee for target practice after work that day. "I know if anybody was kind to him that he would be happy about it because as you know the stories, that very few people had been kind to the boy. I—I'm not bitter about that, but I mean, he—he liked to be alone; I'm somewhat that way myself, but if anybody shows me any kindness, I'm joyous about it, I'd be thankful for it. . . ."

"Then what do you have to say about the reported witnesses who placed your son, armed with a pistol, at the theater and also at the place where Officer Tippit was shot?"

"Well now about Officer Tippit, I'm not sure about that, and there's a lot of people not sure about that either. And I don't care to go into it, but, ha-ha, who is Officer Tippit? Who was Officer Tippit? There's a million questions that come to my mind, and why was Lee so abusive in the theater when he was so calm at the police station after interrogation for so many hours? He still was calm when I saw him; he still was calm when the television audience saw him and [he] said he didn't do it. This whole thing is a frame-up in my opinion, and I am getting reports on the same thing in the papers that are advertising it."

The bellicose little woman wound up her harangue: "I'm going to believe he's innocent because I heard the man say it, and I'm going to believe in the American way of life. And if I'm not to believe that, then I don't belong here; I need to go some other place myself!"

On the heels of that patriotic rant, she changed her voice to a melodic toodledoo: "Well thank you."

After laying groundwork for a possible sound-on-film interview that never took place, I hung up the phone shaking my head at Marguerite Oswald's dizzying illogic. Her coldness struck me. She seemed without grief, filled instead with outrage—icy, edgy, and spoiling to argue.

Firm in her own role as a mistreated loner, she'd borne a son who'd followed her solitary model. When police arrested him, the lone woman had relied on the *Fort Worth Star-Telegram's* Bob Schieffer for a ride to Dallas Police headquarters. Our Steve Pieringer had filmed reporters carrying her boy's coffin to its grave. Attendants had asked their help because Lee Oswald had no friends to serve as pallbearers.

ON THE SCENE

5
Moving with the Story

GEORGE PHENIX

"This is not a gun."

That's the first thing I said to a Secret Service agent who checked our press credentials at Love Field. With all the tension, I wanted to make certain he knew the microphone, which had a pistol grip and a long barrel, was truly a microphone. After all, I was going to be pointing it at the president as he and Jacqueline greeted the awaiting crowd at the airport. The Secret Service man smiled; he was familiar with the unfortunately named shotgun mike. We were all edgy about the right-wing nuts after the Adlai Stevenson incident a month before.

George "Sandy" Sanderson and I were assigned to film the president and first lady as they landed at Love Field. Sandy ran the camera, and I was his sound man for this leg of our coverage. Somehow I managed to shoot some silent footage while monitoring the cumbersome sound gear.

Sandy was an original. In his late sixties, he was the oldest cameraman in Dallas and one of the best. Sandy had operated motion picture cameras since the old hand-cranked days and had worked for Dallas film companies, shooting all sorts of subjects from commercials to advertising and training films.

Although Sandy had a gruff exterior, he mentored many a young cameraman, me included. And he knew everybody. Earle Cabell, then mayor of Dallas and soon to be congressman, had a special nickname for Sandy: "Goat." The two had grown up together, and the mayor remembered when the young George Sanderson had a little wagon pulled by a pet goat. The name stuck. I can't imagine where he got the name Sandy.

I got goose bumps as the Kennedys shook hands with well-wishers who pressed against the chain-link fence just to get closer to JFK. He was the first president I had seen in person. He was strong. She was beautiful. Besides, I had been a reporter for only about six weeks. That's not long enough to get jaded.

Maybe everybody in the crowd got goose bumps. Camelot had come to Dallas.

But they didn't stay long at the airport. As the presidential motorcade left the airport, Sandy and I headed toward the Trade Mart, my next assignment. I put fresh film into my 16 mm Bell and Howell and gave Sandy the roll I had shot at the airport. Sandy was picking up film from others stationed along the motorcade route, and he was to leapfrog to another location later on.

Things are going well, I thought, when Sandy dropped me off into the huge crowd outside the Trade Mart. Friendly-looking. No protestors that I could see. Sandy turned the car back to the station. He was running Pony Express and dropping off our film along with someone else's before picking up his next assignment. My job was to wait outside and film the president leaving the Trade Mart after his speech. With time to kill, I worked my way through the crowd to get in position for the best camera angle. I smoked nervously and made small talk with some of the crowd.

In the distance, I heard sirens. Lots of sirens. Was the commotion coming from the motorcade? I could barely see the vehicles on the expressway in the distance, but I could see enough to know there were multiple vehicles. And it sounded like every car had a siren wailing. We milled around a bit. I was jumpy, but then again, I'm usually jumpy. Suddenly, a lady in the crowd started crying. "He's been hit," she sobbed. "He's been hit." She'd been listening to our radio broadcasts.

"Who?" I asked.

"The president. He's been hit."

"With what?" I asked. Rock? Bottle? Brick? I never thought bullet.

I had no way of knowing, but inside the Trade Mart, Eddie Barker was breaking the news to the nation that the president had been shot. Governor Connally, too.

Out of the corner of my eye, I spotted a uniformed air force officer sprinting to his waiting car and driver. I caught him as he was opening the door. "Where are you going?" I asked.

"Parkland Hospital," he shouted back.

"Me, too," I said, instinctively diving into the back seat with him. We were hauling at ninety miles per hour on the same route our mortally wounded president had taken moments before.

"They shot him," the officer roared, slamming his fist on the back of the front seat. "They shot the son of a bitch." I asked who had been shot. I still didn't know what had happened back at Dealey Plaza. I only knew something bad, really bad, was coming down.

"They shot the president," he said. Then, all of a sudden, I came into focus. For the first time, the officer realized I was in his car and was headed to Parkland along with him. For one brief instant, I truly believe he considered throwing me out of the car—without asking the driver to pull over first. He was not happy that his hitchhiker was a reporter. He got quiet and so did I. Perhaps we both were thinking about what's next. I had no idea what I was getting into.

When we got to the hospital, dignitaries and reporters who had been riding in the motorcade were milling around the emergency entrance. I ran up and got some footage of roses in the floorboard of one of the limousines from the motorcade. I felt like a ghoul invading someone's grief.

George Phenix (upper left) questions motorcade participants outside Parkland Hospital. *Photograph courtesy The Sixth Floor Museum at Dealey Plaza.* Dallas Times Herald *Collection*

Within moments, the Secret Service came out and demanded that the press move away from the emergency entrance. The spot they picked was out of camera range for me, so I bolted from the pack and ran toward the hospital. I wondered if I would get shot. Fortunately, the door was open on the wing overlooking the emergency entrance. Quickly, I ran up a flight of stairs to the second floor and burst into the room of some unknown patient. "Press," I said, "I need that window."

To my amazement, several people standing at the window moved to give me room. They had been watching the unfolding drama, and someone encouraged me to "get up there and get the pictures." Five or six people were sharing that window with me. At least one was a nurse. One might have been the patient, but I had no idea who the others were. We were all caught up in the terrible moment. And I got the distinct impression that my temporary roommates wanted me to get that part of history down on film.

I filmed Jackie as she got into the hearse that would carry her and her husband's body back to Air Force One. She had come to Dallas as first lady; she was leaving as a new widow. I could see red stains contrasting on her pink dress. Later, I learned it was her husband's blood.

Outside, I hooked up with my colleague Dan Garza. Dan, a writer of short stories, usually was an easygoing guy. But this time he was blunt. "Where the hell have you been?" he asked. "Everyone at the station was worried about you." In my rush to get footage, I had completely forgotten to let anyone know where I was. Worse, I forgot that we were also a radio station. I had not filed a single report. I could only hope that older, wiser heads from the station were also there.

Fortunately, they were. Warren Fulks and Bob Huffaker were on the scene near the rear of the hospital. Bob had broadcast the motorcade and had arrived at Parkland with Warren before I did. They had already set up a broadcast routine using the two-way in the little black Mercury news wagon. Thank God. Warren and Bob would be closest to the action around the hospital emergency room. Not only did they broadcast the sad scene at the hospital and report Governor Connally's condition, they did double duty back at the station, writing and reporting their eyewitness observations from the studios.

Dan Garza was in contact with the station via the two-way, and we were told to haul as quickly as we could to Love Field. He was driving, and he began jumping curbs in the news wagon as we raced to get out

The hearse backs up to Parkland Hospital bearing the casket for the president's body. *Photograph courtesy The Sixth Floor Museum at Dealey Plaza.* Dallas Times Herald *Collection*

of Parkland and on the way to Love Field. Dan figured someone would be summoned to swear in LBJ as president. I was only thinking about shooting more film. Shooting film: that was the only thing real to me at the moment. Shooting film.

When we arrived back at Love Field, police wouldn't allow us anywhere near Air Force One. Inside the curtained airliner, Federal Judge Sarah T. Hughes administered the oath of office to LBJ as they stood beside the murdered president's blood-smeared widow.

THE HATEFUL GENERAL

On the day of JFK's visit, we'd all been nervous with good reason, because recent history was on the side of tragedy. Barely a month had passed since Ambassador Adlai Stevenson had been struck with a protestor's sign, and I too had been brushed with the violence of the same so-called National Indignation Convention.

A week or so before the president's trip to Dallas, Alabama Governor George Wallace was speaking at the Baker Hotel. Although I was in the hotel on another story, Eddie Barker had instructed me to help Dan

Garza film the governor when I completed my assignment. When I got to the ballroom, Wallace was already speaking. I tiptoed up to Dan and asked how I could help. He pointed out former General Edwin Walker in the audience and told me to go get some silent footage of him. And he reminded me that we were shooting for CBS. Talk about pressure. I had been on the job five weeks and already I was shooting for CBS. This was the same General Walker that Lee Oswald had tried to kill the previous April. At this time, that attempted murder was still unsolved.

Carefully, because I had a fifteen-pound battery slung by a strap over my shoulder, I made my way through the packed audience to get to the general. I held the battery to keep it from banging someone in the head and meandered up to General Walker. As I turned my light on, he stood up and said, "I've had enough of this. Get out of here."

Fresh out of journalism school, I said the only thing I knew to say: "One more picture." Bad choice of words.

The general grabbed my light, which, naturally, was hooked to my camera. He was six-foot-four, and I was five-eleven. I managed to reach out in space and grab everything back, but I was off balance and twisting away from him. He took advantage of the opportunity and hit me in the back with both fists, knocking me over a tray of stacked luncheon dishes, which clattered to the floor.

Dan's camera was locked down onto Governor Wallace, who had a peculiar nervous gesture. The whole time of the fight, he never said a word but picked his nose constantly.

The general knocked me down two more times, and I scurried to get out of his line of attack. My battery pack was swinging wildly, and I worried about cracking someone's head open. As I reached the end of the row of tables, I tossed the camera, light, and battery pack on the table and turned around with the best haymaker I could muster. Too late— the general was already on his way back to his table.

Days later I figured out what had set him off. Before I got there, the local press corps had been pestering him for pictures and a statement. He must have thought I was one of them coming back for seconds.

The crowd of two thousand right-wingers applauded the general. It scared the hell out of me. When I returned to the station with my great story, Eddie Barker chewed me out for not getting film of Walker pummeling me. It wouldn't happen again. Two more times that year, I got in altercations and managed to get film both times.

After the hectic Friday of the assassination, Saturday and Sunday were a blur. At least twice the station sent me to the melee on the third floor of the police department. It got pretty rough as hundreds of reporters, cameramen, sound men and technicians jockeyed for space. Only a couple of women reporters were covering the story. After a few hours up there, you remembered what it was like to lose a fight. Once while I was rewinding my camera, I accidentally hit some guy in the head with the handle. Hit him pretty hard. As I apologized, he said, "No sweat. I'll get you the next time." The out-of-town media were tough.

ROUGH TIMES AT THE COURTHOUSE

During the opening days of Jack Ruby's trial, rumors were flying that Melvin Belli, Ruby's attorney, was going to rouse protestors to march on the Dallas County Courthouse. Perhaps because I was the youngest reporter in our newsroom, I was assigned to patrol the city block surrounding the courthouse. It was still winter, freezing at about seventeen degrees. There were at least three entrances to the courthouse, so I had to walk fast to cover all three. At least it kept me warm.

After I had made my rounds several times, I saw a taxi pull up on the north side. I recognized the woman. It was Ruby's sister, Eva Grant. But the man was a stranger to me.

Not for long. He barreled out of the cab, a bundle of hate and anger headed straight for me. Having learned my lesson, this time I was ready. I was working with a steel-jacketed Bell & Howell 16 mm movie camera. It was tough as a tank. As one of Ruby's three brothers threw a punch at my face, I managed to block his fist with the camera. It turned out to be a great shot—the furious brother charging at the camera, face contorted, throwing a punch straight into the lens. Everything faded to black. The film sequence was dramatic, to say the least.

But after I took the punch, I turned the camera around, slapped its hard back against my hand and said, "If you really want this camera, I'll give it to you." He must have believed me. He took off running into the side entrance of the courthouse. And to this day I don't know why, but I chased him inside and up the stairs. We burst into some courtroom, where two deputies grabbed us. I did some fancy talking to get out of that one.

My filming got physical again when two inmates escaped from the county jail during the Ruby trial. One escapee's sister was driving his getaway car, and I was riding with a sheriff's deputy in hot pursuit. The officer at the chase car's wheel was good at intercepting, and he cut her off, brought her to a stop, and blocked her escape. Her brother had managed to jump out unseen, but she was not happy to see us and came at me yelling, scratching and kicking. I was about to defend myself at her expense when, out of the corner of my eye, I noticed a reporter from another Dallas station shooting her attacking me. Preferring not to make any news of my own, I covered up and took it until the deputy pulled her off.

Later, back at the county jail, I was filming the mop-up after the jailbreak. Sheriff Bill Decker was pulling off his wet shoes and socks after officers had used a water hose to quell a threatening riot among the prisoners. The sheriff noticed that the wristband on his watch was stretched out of shape.

"Did you get it caught on a jail cell?" I asked.

"Hell no," the sixty-five-year-old sheriff said. "I hit the son of a bitch with my left."

MY SHOT AT OSWALD

On the day Oswald was to be transferred from the city to the county jail, my phone rang at four in the morning. It was someone at the station telling me to get my butt down there as fast as I could. I was going to be part of the team covering the transfer.

Most of the good equipment was in use elsewhere. We couldn't find a tripod for me to mount the camera. A shaky unipod would have to do. To this day, I hate unipods.

Wes Wise, a versatile reporter who was also our ten o'clock sportscaster, helped me load the news wagon. Then Wes drove me to the police station, dropped me in the basement garage, and headed for the county jail to meet Oswald's arrival there. About nine that Sunday morning we drove into the basement, unchallenged, down the same ramp Jack Ruby would use a few hours later. There were policemen in the basement, and we were driving a well-marked news wagon. But nobody asked for an ID.

Since I had first choice, I picked the spot where my lens would be looking straight down the path where Lee Harvey Oswald would be paraded toward us. Slowly, the media crowd began to gather. Bob Huf-faker tucked the CBS mike into his coat pocket while he helped me reach the overhead pipes where I strung my mike.

We waited.

Suddenly Oswald was coming through the jail office door flanked by big detectives. It was happening fast. I had Oswald centered in my viewfinder when—*ka-bam*. We were essentially in a cement box when Ruby's gun went off, and it was really loud. My reflexes won over my news judgment, and my head jerked up from the viewfinder. The camera lurched on that blasted unipod. Later, Dean Angel, our chief film editor, timed the frames I'd lost. I had regained control in five seconds, but it had seemed to me like an eternity while I struggled against the surge of reporters and police. At one point, I saw a lawman hurdle over a car to get into the fray. The police were fighting to keep Ruby from squeezing off another round, and they won by sheer force of numbers. Several brave men jumped into that pile.

Hurriedly they took Oswald back inside the building while the melee went on. Police were protecting the area with their bodies. Lots of yelling—pandemonium is a mild description.

When they wheeled Oswald out toward the ambulance, I thought he was already dead. His head wobbled as the stretcher rolled over the uneven cement floor. His face was already ashen. He was dying of massive internal bleeding, and it took a few crucial seconds to move the armored truck from the exit ramp so that the ambulance could get out of the basement.

Ironically, once the armored truck moved and the ambulance sped up and out of the garage, my troubles began. The police sealed the area. Nobody could leave unless they could prove they had a legitimate reason to be in the basement in the first place. My problem? I was so new that I had not been issued permanent press credentials. Although I had been issued credentials for the president's trip, they were useless after that terrible day.

It looked like I was going to be stuck in the basement, but a policeman recognized me. He remembered me from earlier in the week when I had driven the wrong way down a one-way street in front of Neiman Marcus. That day, he had whistled me to the curb, pointed out the one-way signs and asked, "Son, you want to report news—or make news?"

Once I was free of the basement, I searched for a phone. I needed a

George Phenix, at right, among reporters at police headquarters. *Photograph courtesy The Sixth Floor Museum at Dealey Plaza.* Dallas Times Herald *Collection*

ride back to the station. Sorry, they said. All our mobile units are on the way to Parkland Hospital—again.

I thought I might have some hot film, so I managed to load my 129-pound body with all my gear: the big camera, unipod, microphone, cable, battery, and who knows what else. Outside the jail building, I stepped into the middle of Main Street. Traffic screeched, and one good citizen, a total stranger, offered me a ride back to KRLD.

We put the film in the developing process, and Eddie Barker called the FBI. I paced and smoked and waited for the film to be developed. The night before, I had loaded the film wrong and ruined an exclusive interview that CBS reporter Nelson Benton had grabbed with Police Chief Curry.

Anxiously I watched as Dean Angel threaded the film through the projector. "Please, God, let there be at least some sort of image on the film." I knew if anyone could pull the film through the long line of developing tanks intact it would be Dean. He was calm under pressure. More than once, he had saved my hide by getting an image despite poor photography.

The film finally came out of the soup and there Jack Ruby was, standing just off my right shoulder. He stepped in front of my camera and—bang.

I walked out of the screening room, shaken. I would see my film only one more time.

SLOW MOTION: SEEDS OF A CONSPIRACY THEORY

Dan Rather narrated my film as it flickered before the national viewing audience on the afternoon of November 24: "Now we will show you the film of Oswald being shot, still-framed," Rather says. "Watch the hat in the right-hand corner of the frame. Watch Oswald's eyes as they seem to catch the eye of the assassin [Ruby]. His head turns, he looks at the assassin and his eyes never leave him. The assassin moves in . . . and a few inches from [Oswald's] abdomen, fires a shot."

Rather's speculation spawned the enduring theory that Oswald recognized his killer—though the assassin was glancing at a New York reporter who, violating our agreement with the police neither to move nor question Oswald, walked up and confronted him a split second before Ruby fired.

I never saw my film again. Since the station hadn't given me a copy, I sneaked in around midnight weeks later and developed my own. When we moved back to Austin a year later, the film wound up in my chest of drawers, where my four-year-old son Steven and three-year-old daughter Leann found it one day. They imagined it to be some sort of new kind of yo-yo and repeatedly rolled it up and down the hallway—ruined it. I didn't see my own film sequence again for thirty years—in the Sixth Floor Museum at Dealey Plaza.

Images from those nightmarish days are burned into my brain—some of them from my own eyes, others borrowed memories. For four decades, people have asked me whether I thought there was a conspiracy. Now what the hell would a twenty-four-year-old cub reporter fresh out of Lubbock know about a conspiracy? I don't know.

But I do know this: I am proud to have worked with a bunch of local reporters who were taking care of business. We had a job to do even in the face of national sorrow, and we did it. Long hours made us bone-weary at times, but we had a responsibility to get the news out to a grieving nation. I remember I didn't get a chance to cry over President Kennedy until days later when I finally got some time off. Sometimes even now, when I think of the Kennedy family, I cry again.

6

Gunman, Mob, and Mourners

BILL MERCER

Kneeling in the police basement assembly room after midnight, I looked up directly into the face of the man accused of killing President John F. Kennedy. Here was Lee Harvey Oswald at his peculiar showing before the press. Hundreds of reporters from all over the United States and some from foreign countries were pressed shoulder to shoulder, trying to ask the question of this former U.S. Marine, former resident of Russia, who it was alleged had pulled the trigger on his Mannlicher-Carcano 6.5 rifle three times. He had been hunkered down in his window seat on the sixth floor of the Texas School Book Depository overlooking the presidential motorcade as it was leaving downtown Dallas: right from Main onto Houston Street, then slowly down onto Elm at the triple underpass. The second of his bullets struck the president and wounded Governor John Connally. The first, deflected by a tree, had struck the south curb of Main Street. The third and final shot tore off part of the president's head.

Nonetheless, Oswald seemed perfectly at ease as questions were fired at him. Had he shot the president? Had he shot Patrolman J. D. Tippit? Who was he working for? Why did he want to kill the president? On and on went the questions for several minutes. I was not concerned about asking any while the media gang hurled theirs at this man with the bruised face. "A policeman hit me" was his answer to how the obvious blow to his face occurred. As police concluded the "press conference" and Oswald started to turn, I stood up with the mike in my hand. When he was again asked, "Did you kill the president?" Oswald looked toward me and said, "No, I have not been charged with that. In fact, nobody has said that to me yet. The first thing I heard about it was when the newspaper reporters in the hall asked me that question." He pronounced it "axed." I looked into his face and said, "You have been charged." Oswald looked a little blank and moved his head backward in a natural reflective response. And then he was taken back to his cell on the fifth floor. Sunday he would be dead.

LOW-TECH NEWS

The KRLD radio and TV newsroom of the 1960s had little resemblance to high-tech news operations of the twenty-first century. We covered news with hand-held 16 mm film cameras and huge sound film cameras. No quick turnaround video cameras as today. No satellites for instant reporting from the scene. Take a film camera, shoot the story, run it back to the newsroom, have it processed, write the story, and time its phrases with a stopwatch to fit the film's shots to the copy. Often you'd edit the film yourself, measuring the length of each shot to fit the number of seconds called for by the narrative. As you cut the

Bill Mercer and KRLD cameraman Gene Pasczalek (upper right) advance toward Oswald at the midnight press showing. *Photograph courtesy The Sixth Floor Museum at Dealey Plaza.* Dallas Times Herald *Collection*

pieces that would make the story, you stuck them temporarily to the edge of the editing table, then glued them together—as fast as possible if you were racing to the deadline.

My college degree was in journalism and radio, and I had worked in newspaper and radio news before coming to KRLD, where I specialized in sports play-by-play broadcasting. When I wasn't chasing football, baseball and basketball games with my microphone and movie camera, I was a reporter and newscaster on both radio and television. All of the KRLD News staff did everything. Like the rest, I covered news, shot film, interviewed, dug up stories, did investigative reporting—all the essential jobs in the news business.

COMMENT

Our news director, Eddie Barker, wanted versatility, and I also was part of the interview crew on the first interview-talk show in Dallas: *Comment*. The program was Eddie's successful idea—and a pioneering step in talk radio. Every day was a thrill, sitting in with Barker, Frank Glieber, Jim Underwood, and Wes Wise. We would interview a newsmaker for thirty minutes and then have listeners call in with questions and comments. The program brought in every prominent businessman and politician in the Dallas–Fort Worth area, in addition to guests like Dr. Edward Teller, Billy Graham, Alabama Governor George Wallace, Black Panther spokesmen, George Bush the elder, Ginger Rogers, Robert Goulet, and even Colonel Sanders.

But we also occasionally had guests who claimed to have credentials while also claiming that just about everyone in government was a Communist or a sympathizer. What emerged was a stark recognition of the tumult of the times. There was the group headed by General Edwin Walker, the John Birch Society, and others who were clamoring against President Kennedy in the aftermath of the McCarthy hearings. They sensed Communists around every corner; the administration was "soft on Communism" and worse. The right-wingers railed against foreign troops on our native soil, and they complained that foreign aviators were being trained at airfields north of Dallas. They thought that the United Nations and various subversives were destroying our democracy, our government. It was a hectic time, and some of our *Comment* programs required strong journalistic procedures. More than once we demanded that some guest either prove insubstantial allegations with facts and figures or leave the program. Long on zeal and short on evidence, a few of them walked out.

With this almost daily buildup of tension, then the vocal and physical attacks on United Nations Ambassador Adlai Stevenson when he spoke a month earlier in Dallas, the approaching visit of President Kennedy worried us.

I was also the newscaster on Channel 4's noon news. We were not known as "anchors." I rewrote copy, edited film, wrote breaking stories, edited in new film stories, and then typed the format with all the film cues and commercial breaks. Then I delivered the whole newscast on the air.

THE END OF CAMELOT

The evening before President Kennedy's visit, I was driving back to Dallas after teaching a radio journalism class at North Texas State University in Denton, thirty-five miles to the north. Thinking of JFK's arrival the next day gave me some chills. I wasn't worried about his physical safety, but like my colleagues, I feared that some of the strongest anti-Kennedy groups would somehow embarrass him and his entourage. Ambassador Stevenson had been heckled and struck with a placard, and a nasty advertisement against Kennedy had appeared in the *Dallas Morning News*. I could not imagine what might happen—maybe huge signs, people throwing things. A gut feeling was churning around that Kennedy would be insulted by one of the highly charged groups in Dallas.

On November 22 every reporter in our newsroom was out on the story: Frank Glieber and film cameramen at Dallas Love Field, where the presidential plane would land; Jim Underwood riding in the caravan of cars that would parade through downtown; Wes Wise and Bob Huffaker along the motorcade route; and Eddie Barker at the Trade Mart, where Kennedy was to speak. There were pool cameras live at the airport and with Eddie at the Trade Mart. Using mobile units' two-way radios, Frank would broadcast the Love Field arrival, and Wes and Bob would broadcast the motorcade, but everything else was covered by film cameras. The entire staff was on the story, and I was left preparing the noon newscast in an empty newsroom. After delivering the noon news, I left the television studio and returned to a newsroom that broke into turmoil at the news of a shooting in the motorcade. People were crying, screaming. Everything was chaos. It was thought the president was injured.

Throughout the afternoon we were busy answering calls from all over the nation and from overseas. I had a direct line open to a radio station in Boston. We couldn't answer all the questions. Slowly the facts filtered in, and finally from the Trade Mart came Eddie's message that President Kennedy was dead.

The emotional pressure was enormous. It was difficult not to choke up when talking to these earnest people on the various telephone connections, especially the Massachusetts stations. This bothered me for a long time afterward, but knowing that Walter Cronkite had suffered this reaction on the air to the story made it easier to accept.

Reporters and cameramen—no women in those days—roared into the newsroom, developing film, writing stories, doing radio "voicers" about what they had seen. It was six hours of tumult and a mad dash to put the story together for the six o'clock newscasts on TV and radio.

THE MOB AT POLICE HEADQUARTERS

After the six o'clock newscasts were done, we had a newsroom meeting, at which I received my first assignment: cover the action at the Dallas Police Department's third-floor offices. The KRLD-TV engineering department was placing one of those huge black-and-white studio cameras on the third floor of the building so that a continuous picture could be microwaved back to the station. I was the guy with the microphone.

When Sergeant Jerry Hill and other officers brought Lee Harvey Oswald from the Texas Theater into police headquarters that afternoon, they were trailed by a score of local photographers and news reporters who had followed the progress of the story with the police. As they escorted Oswald into the building, photographers raced ahead taking pictures and actually rode in the elevator as it took Oswald to the third floor. Such open press access was routine in Dallas when someone was arrested in a high-profile case. When I arrived at the Dallas Police and Courts Building's third floor shortly before seven o'clock that evening, reporters and photographers were steadily gathering. Some had been

Oswald is escorted through a hallway at police headquarters. *Photograph courtesy The Sixth Floor Museum at Dealey Plaza. Photographer Bill Winfrey, the* Dallas Morning News. *Tom Dillard Collection.*

there since early afternoon when police first brought Oswald in for questioning.

Several times that afternoon, Oswald stood in lineups in the basement assembly room, where he would endure a news conference after midnight. Before his first appearance, officers searched him and found five .38 bullets in his pocket. Then began a series of journeys to Captain Will Fritz's office on the third floor and back downstairs to lineups. Shortly after seven o'clock that evening, police charged Oswald with murdering Patrolman Tippit. Oswald was formally arraigned before Justice of the Peace David L. Johnston in Captain Fritz's office. Then Oswald was back in the lineup basement room, and our big cameras caught him on tape when he returned to the third floor for more interrogation in the homicide office. The official complaint charging Oswald with the murder of President Kennedy was signed at 11:26 P.M.

The third floor of the old building, constructed in the 1920s, housed the main offices of the Dallas Police Department. The public elevators opened into a lobby at the midpoint of a corridor that extended the length of the floor, about 140 feet. The corridor was narrow, only about seven feet wide. At one end of the hallway were the offices of Dallas Chief of Police Jesse E. Curry and his assistants, and at the other end was a small pressroom that could accommodate just a handful of reporters. Along the corridor were other police offices, the various detective bureaus, and the homicide and robbery bureau, headed by Captain Fritz.

Patrolman Tippit had been killed, the suspect Oswald had been apprehended in the Texas Theater in Oak Cliff, and how all of this came together was an amazing saga that hundreds of reporters from around the nation were trying to sort out. More were arriving with every landing at Love Field.

The homicide offices were down the hall from our camera, and I stretched a microphone cable the length of the building as close to the wall as possible from the south end to the north, where everyone

Bill Mercer interviews homicide captain Will Fritz between his sessions of questioning Oswald. *Photograph courtesy The Sixth Floor Museum at Dealey Plaza.* Dallas Times Herald *Collection*

congregated. As the evening progressed, that cable and I were all over the place.

Just after I'd taken my appointed spot at the end of the building where the actors in this drama would be coming and going, an extremely wide-bodied person with a number of still cameras draped over his torso approached me and asked what that cable on the floor was. I explained the production plan, and he told me that if the cable got in his way he would yank it out. I replied that if he did I would bring my foot-long microphone down on his head. Shortly after that our six-foot-plus engineer, Howard Chamberlain, ambled up and asked if there was a problem. I assured him there was no problem, now. This was seat-of-the-pants television reporting. There was no director, except Leigh Webb in our van outside on Commerce Street, and Benny Molina, our floor director who guarded the cameraman and stayed in contact with Leigh and with CBS in New York.

Whenever some official person I recognized came out of an office or off the elevator, I moved in with questions. After a few such sorties, the out-of-town reporters began to realize that the guy with the microphone was familiar with these various people. Then as the evening progressed, the reporting crowd grew larger and hovered over everybody I approached. I was joined by Nelson Benton, a CBS reporter who had flown in with Dan Rather's crew. Nelson stuck by my side the entire evening.

I was on the alert, as were the other reporters, for arrivals or departures of District Attorney Henry Wade and his assistant Bill Alexander, Chief of Police Jesse Curry, Homicide Captain Will Fritz, Captain Glen D. King, administrative assistant to Curry, and Sergeant Jerry Hill, one of our close associates at the department, who did traffic reporting for KRLD radio. Officer Nick McDonald showed me where the hammer of Oswald's pistol had hit the skin between his thumb and forefinger as he grasped the gun to keep it from firing when he jumped Oswald in the theater. I didn't interview one particular man who was among us at police headquarters that night: the strip-club operator Jack Ruby.

Some reporters had been in the corridor since two o'clock that afternoon. These represented the local papers and radio and television stations, with whom the Dallas police had a professional, cordial and respectful relationship. Given the tradition of cooperation between police and the local press, officials were initially unconcerned about re-

CBS reporter Nelson Benton (left) beside Chief Jesse Curry (upper left) questions Capt. Will Fritz (in hat) and District Attorney Henry Wade outside the homicide office Friday night. *Photograph courtesy The Sixth Floor Museum at Dealey Plaza.* Dallas Times Herald *Collection*

porters being on the third floor observing and throwing questions at the suspect, his family, and officers. But from seven o'clock that evening the throng of outside news representatives rose to three hundred or more in that narrow corridor. Oswald was moved through the crowd of reporters numerous times between the homicide office and the locked door leading to the jail elevator.

The accused assassin was always surrounded by several detectives. The press threw him questions, and he answered rather calmly.

"Did you kill the president?"

"I didn't kill anybody."

"How did you get that bruise on your face?"

"A policeman hit me."

He faced furious outbursts of questions while he was walking with his escort of detectives. Chief Curry came into the hallway and presented statements, answered questions, and cooperated with the increasingly aggressive multitude. District Attorney Wade also appeared at least twice, and he too answered the press. A detective came down the hall holding aloft Oswald's Mannlicher-Carcano 6.5 rifle, which was alleged to be the murder weapon. This turned out to be one of those dramatic pictures that stayed in the film or video highlight reel.

Each time the elevator or a door in the offices opened we headed into the fray, thrusting the microphone in to pick up answers, while our cameraman kept a cool head and focused on the subject. The narrow third-floor hallway became so congested and the reporters so aggressive that detectives and other officials had trouble opening office doors. At times they had to push their way physically through the noisy media.

I stood in front of one office door waiting to interview an official who was due to emerge, but when he started out, the news crowd surged forward and the opening door swept me in behind it, totally out of sight. Later I saw the videotape, which showed me still there when the door closed again. The mob of reporters was gradually overwhelming a police department that had never faced anything like this, as it tried to give us access to the accused.

Oswald's pretty Russian-born wife Marina arrived with their daughter in her arms, accompanied by his mother, Marguerite Oswald. They seemed oblivious to questions hurled at them. Marina seemed dismayed by the affair, while Marguerite displayed a strong and defiant attitude. The pandemonium went on throughout the more than five hours I was

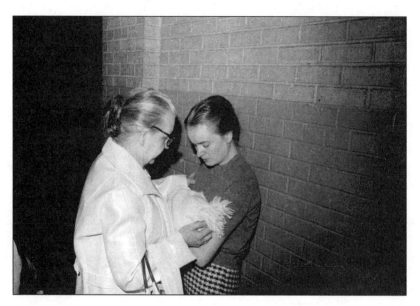

Oswald's estranged wife, Marina, holds their infant as she and the assassin's mother, Marguerite, leave police headquarters through the basement. *Photograph courtesy The Sixth Floor Museum at Dealey Plaza.* Dallas Times Herald *Collection*

stationed there. At one point I was caught in the mass of pushing re-porters, uttering, "I am being pummeled, I am being pummeled." It was not a pretty sight.

Today it is unthinkable that such a mob of news people, myself in-cluded, could be in such proximity to the accused, but under pressure from the press, police were trying to show that Oswald was not being mistreated, though his face had been bruised during the arrest. State-ments made by different officials that night also proved the police were attempting to follow correct procedures of interrogation and then pass-ing on their findings to the assembled press. Chief Curry made some fifteen statements to the media on Friday and Saturday. Captain Fritz was less frequently interviewed but answered some questions pre-sented to him. If all of this was not great journalism, certainly from our point of view it kept the nation informed. Then the dramatic climax to this terrible day of assassination, murder and arrest: just before Friday's midnight, District Attorney Wade announced that Oswald would ap-pear shortly at a news conference in the basement assembly room.

Our KRLD-TV engineers somehow lugged their huge camera down-stairs, pulled the cable into the basement, and were set up with the picture before the press stampeded into the room. The assembly room had a stage with a one-way nylon cloth screen used to prevent suspects in a lineup from seeing witnesses identifying them. The screen prevented the cameras from taking pictures of anyone behind it, so Oswald was to be placed on the floor below the stage.

At least a hundred members of the press, reporters and photographers of every ilk, were in the small room. Later it would be confirmed that Jack Ruby was in attendance. When Oswald was escorted in, the room became a cacophony of questions, demands to sit down in front, general mayhem. I edged forward until I was kneeling on the floor directly below Oswald so that my mike could pick up his responses to questions he chose to answer. The press throng were in no way civil to the suspect or to each other, and after about two minutes Chief Curry ordered Oswald out of the room. That was when I stood so that our mike could pick up his answer—and when I informed him that he had been charged with assassinating the president. Following Oswald's departure there was a feeling like that of air being sucked from the atmosphere after an explosion.

The developing tragedy was now entering the early minutes of Saturday morning, and on Sunday Oswald would be dead. Bob Huffaker and George Phenix, along with our cameraman Jim English and floor director Bob Hankal, would be in the police garage to broadcast television's first murder.

CONFESSION AMONG FLOWERS

On Monday following Jack Ruby's one-shot killing of Oswald, we were conferring in the newsroom about his motive, his connections to anyone who might have wanted Oswald dead, puzzling over the bizarre turn of events. Ruby probably had some mob connections; that was one of the assumptions that came out of our discussion. The Dallas–Fort Worth area had a number of high-profile gang-type gamblers, club owners, and con men. And there had been some murders in connection with these folks.

I knew one contact in Dallas who I figured would know about any connections, if any, between Ruby and organized crime. So I called him and told him that I was investigating Ruby's possible connection to any group that might have encouraged him to shoot Oswald. He said he couldn't talk about anything like that. I promised him anonymity if he could only give me some idea whom I might ask. Predictably and politely, he said there was no way that he could provide information about Ruby or anyone else. He added that he was sorry he couldn't help and hung up. To this day I believe that he would have known about Ruby's connections with any gang-related operations. I'd made him an offer he could refuse. As for Ruby, it would have been odd for the mob to rely on such a public groupie as a hit man.

There was a story that some Dallas schoolchildren had cheered when the announcement was made that school was to be dismissed because the president had been killed. It wasn't clear whether it had happened at all—or if it had, whether the children had reacted only to the news that they were to be let out of classes. But the story had, as they say, legs. This was Dallas with its reputation destroyed—a cesspool of right-wing hatred, a town that "killed" the president. Many journalists were blaming the city, often with the words "disgrace" and "shame."

Eddie Barker strongly doubted the allegation, which a tipster had called in as true. Barker knew and distrusted the source. He warned Dan Rather away from the story and told him, "Frankly, we don't need that." Eddie felt assured that Dan had agreed not to use it, but then Rather fed it to CBS anyway, and CBS aired it.

Eddie, known for a fiery temper that at times resulted in trash cans being kicked around the office, blew his stack and evicted Rather and the CBS crew from our newsroom, where they had been headquartered.

KRLD News countered the story by arranging for me to interview one of the school's teachers live during our six o'clock newscast. Conducting the five-minute interview, I asked the questions everyone would have. Did the children applaud the announcement of the president's death? Did they applaud when school was cancelled? The teacher calmly denied that the children in her school had reacted to the president's death with anything but the sorrow we all shared. She knew of no other school where it might have happened. If it had occurred, the entire school system would have known.

There were all sorts of rumors about students and their reactions. I was told, after the first story appeared, by a man who swore it was true, that the afternoon of the assassination a youngster banged on his door, weeping, wanting to know where his father was. The boy was sure his father had been involved with the killing, because his father hated Kennedy. Forty years later I mentioned this episode to a friend in another state, and he could give me chapter and verse about the "applauding students."

The story didn't go away. But after negotiations the CBS team came back to the KRLD newsroom. Dallas was damned across the country and overseas: Dallas had created the atmosphere for hate groups to prosper. Dallas hated President Kennedy. Dallas provided the environment for Oswald to plan his attack. Dallas leaders probably were involved in the assassination. These indictments were staggering.

AMONG THE WREATHS

But I covered the outpouring of grief and sympathy by Dallas citizens. Expressions of love and sorrow came from folks throughout the city and every part of Texas. Their tributes were joined by those from other states, and the nation's sentiment became apparent at the infamous triple underpass area, the grassy knoll, the book depository. Thousands of floral wreaths of every size, many handmade, appeared all across the grassy area, covering the assassination site. The curious and the bereaved came to stand, stare and wonder, while a constant city-long procession of cars came down Elm and Main Streets day and night. Forty years later the visitors still come.

The area was beginning to draw hundreds of people as the weekend progressed. There was that constant traffic snarl through the city. The story there spoke of the reaction of Dallas, Texas, and the world to this terrible event. I was chosen to narrate the scene on film.

Neither my cameraman nor I had an easy assignment. Film cameras with sound were large and cumbersome things. And unfortunately the film was black and white—unfortunate because it couldn't reveal the grandeur of the colors of the flowers. Knowing this, I had to describe the colors, the messages, the sadness, the tears, and choke back my own emotion. Imagine bumper-to-bumper traffic cruising by. Imagine hundreds of people standing quietly, some weeping. Imagine thousands of floral tributes with their wrenching messages of despair, love, and anguish. Imagine that and introduce the scene, produce the narration from what you can see and read on the cards, and try to keep your composure.

It was Sunday afternoon when I reported:

Here in Dallas this is the scene where President Kennedy was assassinated on Friday. The people of this city have not been able to pass by the catafalque of the president in Washington, but since the shooting on Friday, the cars have been passing by, lined up from here on West Elm to the east end of the city—a city filled with tragedy. Because the president was killed here, because an officer was killed here, and today the man who shot the president, who was charged with murder, was also shot in Dallas. At first there was one wreath: a wreath on the north side of the street near the triple underpass. And now the flowers have grown to a large display on the south side, as people move in to be curious. To see the spot. To remember the president. They add floral decorations. People are sad in Dallas as they place their mementos.

Then I walked among the various displays reading their messages aloud: "A small American flag draped across the Holy Bible. A card that says only, 'Forgive Us.' There are no smiles here."

Another display with the card, "In memory of our president who we loved dearly." As you walk through this, you feel the hallowedness of the ground now. A red, white, and blue ribbon with the message, "With deepest sympathy. God Forgive us all." This display presented by Falkner, Thompson, Walton, Connelly, and Jeter on behalf of the John Tyler Senior class of 1964, Tyler, Texas. A rosary is draped across the top. A cross with one red rose. A lone carnation: "May you rest in peace."

In the weeks that followed, the floral tributes multiplied to cover every inch of the grassy areas on both sides of Elm Street. Dallas, Texas, and a mourning nation cared.

When we returned to regular programming—*Comment*, in particular—there was a rush of conspiracy theories from listeners and other callers, as well as from some invited guests. Some had crazy ideas about the assassination: who "really" shot the president, phantom shooters who had fled from the grassy knoll. A few called in vowing they had seen gunshots from the grassy knoll, people running and escaping in automobiles. None of them turned out to have seen such things.

One of the first conspiracy notions was that Lyndon Johnson had a hand in it. As I traveled outside Dallas, a cousin in California told me that she was positive about LBJ's involvement, and I met others from California to New York who proclaimed that idea. Others, recalling that Richard Nixon was in town that day, concluded that he had orchestrated the murder. Oh well, Dr. Mudd is still being vilified for treating John Wilkes Booth after he'd shot Abraham Lincoln.

We did not intrude during a funeral ceremony, so when Patrolman Tippit's services were held, I sat in a mobile unit and broadcast the scene as mourners arrived, then as they departed. We were covering all the sadness we could handle.

But one odd assignment tested my instincts and gave me a real feeling of satisfaction. A CBS news producer came to me after the first week of chaos and asked if I would go with their radio sound engineer to the assassination scene and interview a "conservative." That was the request, with no other specifics. As we were driving from the station to the School Book Depository and triple underpass that afternoon, the engineer asked how we were going to know a conservative when we met one. I had no idea, but we were going to try.

The crowd was thinner than usual when we arrived in Dealey Plaza. Sitting up on one of the cement decorations above the grassy knoll was an old black gentleman with a crop of beautiful white hair. He wasn't that so-called conservative we were seeking, but as I talked to him, he gave me a wonderful interview. He was sorry about the people who had been killed, but in a deeply moving message he hurt for all their children: "Young man like that getting killed, besides another policeman. Five kids. What they going to do now?" He talked about the Kennedy children, Tippit's, and particularly Oswald's, who would have to live with his deed. And he wondered about the children who had heard about and lived through this terrible event today in our history and what they would carry with them. "What are we coming to? I don't believe Dallas is at fault. But we get the blame for it," he said, "I don't believe the people of Dallas hated the administration that bad. Some of them might have differed with him in his opinions, naturally, that's so. But all presidents should have a difference of opinion. But not bad enough to murder. As a matter of fact, I couldn't see them spitting on Mr. Stevenson, either. I believe all this stuff is cooked up. I don't believe that's Dallasite stuff. I just don't believe it." It was a touching statement. But the dear man was not a conservative.

The engineer carried his tape recorder slung in front of his chest as he and I walked around greeting people and talking about the tragedy. But we found no one who fit the mold.

Then it happened. We were standing on the Main Street grassy area when I looked up the street toward downtown Dallas. There walking down the small hill was a tall gentleman who obviously was a business type; he wore a gray suit and overcoat with hat to match. He carried a briefcase and an umbrella. If generalities were true he fit the appearance of a more conservative person than we had encountered in the area so far. I decided to allow him plenty of space while I thought through how to approach him. I had to form an introduction and question that would be polite but to the point. I certainly wasn't planning to walk up to him and ask, "Are you a conservative?"

The distinguished-looking man came down the hill and paused at the floral displays. He seemed to read some of their messages as he stood in an attitude of meditation. After a few minutes we walked over to him and I posed my introduction. I introduced myself as a CBS reporter and said, "You appear to be a professional person who has taken some time out of your busy day to come here to the assassination site and I wonder if you could tell us your thoughts?"

His answer was deafeningly honest: "I hated President Kennedy, but I did not wish him dead. I came here today to apologize to him and his family for what happened here." That was a statement I could never forget. "I've been a life-long Republican. That makes no difference. A real great man is gone, and we're all going to suffer for it, and we all should. I just hope that his going helps us to realize what, what sort of thing we have let ourselves fall into—the way we have become. And I hope from this we can take a new birth and realize that we're letting hate undermine us and become too much a part of our life. It doesn't belong in our life."

Eddie Barker had assembled a group of dedicated radio and television professionals. If we weren't professional before the assassination, we certainly achieved that status in the aftermath. Frank Glieber was a sportscaster; Jim Underwood, a weather reporter; Wes Wise was also a sports reporter, as was Eddie. Bob Huffaker did weekend weather and subbed on *Comment*. We were all news reporters and newscasters as well. And these were just a few of my colleagues who carried cameras, covered and wrote stories, interviewed and broadcast daily.

Jim Underwood had been a Marine at Guadalcanal, and I had served three years in the navy, also in the Pacific in World War II. So we were the oldest of this group who served our stations, KRLD-AM-FM-TV, and our public, with the best reporting we could put together. But I felt that I had a minor role in the overall effort. The other staffers were out on the street daily pursuing leads, covering courthouse proceedings, continuing daily interviews with the district attorney, the police and the federal people.

It was an event so overwhelmingly tragic that I hoped no one would ever have to see such a thing happen again. Every day we were emotionally drained from constant pressures of the unfolding stories. The turmoil of the time took its toll on the city. Dallas, as a community, suffered. Later when I traveled on Dallas Cowboys football trips, I met many people in other parts of the country who didn't hesitate to harangue about how terrible Dallas was.

In Dallas there was soul-searching. At a holiday gathering the following month, a lady I knew rushed up in tears, telling me that she was sorry and asking if I could understand that she didn't want the president killed even though she disagreed with him. Somehow she thought of us as counselors who would receive her confession, and she wasn't the only one. Scenes like that happened many times.

We were unlikely confessors, but we were committed to our listeners and viewers. And we tried to tell them the news that mattered, with speed and accuracy. We felt that our mission was to inform our fellow citizens and reassure them that we were there to tell them about history as it happened.

SEEDS OF HATRED

7
The Media, Extremists, and Dallas

WES WISE

Adlai Stevenson, U.S. ambassador to the United Nations, came to Dallas as the featured speaker of the city's U.N. Day observance. It was Thursday, October 24, 1963, a month before JFK's visit.

The fact that Stevenson was hosted by two of the city's best-known "liberals," Federal Judge Sarah T. Hughes and Stanley Marcus, of Neiman-Marcus fame, was not lost to the extreme Dallas right-wing fringe. For several days before the ambassador's scheduled arrival, a loosely organized group calling itself the "National Indignation Convention" busied itself constructing signs for a demonstration at the U.N. gathering. The general theme: "Get the U.S. Out of the U.N."

It fell my duty as president of the Press Club of Dallas to meet the ambassador at noon of U.N. Day on the sidewalk in front of the club, next to the Baker Hotel in the heart of the city. A news conference had been scheduled, and I was relieved that a very respectable contingent of the press was awaiting Stevenson upstairs.

I extended my hand, "Good morning, sir." I was surprised by his small stature and red face. But there was a firm handshake and friendly smile, and the ensuing news conference went exceedingly well.

On his way out of the "Purple Palace," as we Press Club members called our headquarters, Mr. Stevenson turned, waved, and exclaimed, "Thanks for a job well done." But after the flattery, we sensed the first hint of mild unrest as we descended aboard the rickety elevator, where a dozen passengers were packed into the small enclosure. As we stood elbow to elbow, I introduced the ambassador to several people I knew from outside the press. Generally, the meetings were friendly, but as we departed the elevator a man in his thirties muttered loud enough for the ambassador to hear, "What the hell's the United Nations for, anyway?" Little did I know that his comment was a precursor of an event to remember.

Assistant News Director Jim Underwood and I were assigned by News Director Eddie Barker to cover the event. We had discussed in some detail the fact that this would be an unusual opportunity for demonstrations of any persuasion, especially since the program was to be telecast live in the massive Dallas–Fort Worth area.

In those days of news coverage, all of us "doubled in brass"—Underwood was the weatherman, and I was the sports announcer on the ten o'clock news. Our double duties would become a crucial factor later that evening.

As we arrived early at the smallish thousand-seat theater, Jim, with a puzzled look on his face, asked, "What the hell's going on?" Twenty-five or so young men and women, mostly in their twenties, were pacing the foyer bearing anti–United Nations signs and chanting, over and over, "Get the U.S. out of the U.N.!"

We were equipped only with a Bell & Howell 16-mm. camera with a bulky battery pack floodlight attached.

"Jim, I don't like the feel of this," I said. "Did you see how flushed that guy's face was?"

"I don't like this either," Jim answered. "Everyone's sweating and mad."

At least, we agreed, the scene was well staffed with uniformed Dallas policemen. But that judgment was about to be tested. A well-dressed young man waved a large U.S. flag in a wide circular motion, almost striking some fellow demonstrators and bystanders.

"All right!" shouted a cop, "Let's get that American flag outta here!"

"What?" The reaction was predictable and understandable. "You mean to tell me I can't show my patriotism and my love of country by waving my flag? I will not get my American flag outta here!"

The policeman quickly backed off.

Inside the auditorium, as the live locally televised portion of the program was about to begin, Jim and I crouched between the first two rows in front of the stage, which had been reserved for the press. Many of the demonstrators had moved to the balcony, but they continued loud and boisterous.

Finally the dignitaries began filing in to occupy the line of chairs set up onstage. Somehow, the engineers or stagehands had failed to notice that they had set the center portion of the platform about an inch higher than the rest of the stage. As the telecast was about to begin—the "countdown" as we in the business called it—the elevated stage settled with a loud *thump!* visibly jarring the occupants as the stage righted itself.

Did you see that?" Jim exclaimed. "I thought Stevenson's eyes were going to pop right out of his head!"

Yeah," I answered. "I've never seen such a collection of nervous people."

Judge Hughes served as moderator. The din, especially from the balcony, escalated as Ambassador Stevenson began his speech. Finally, he paused in his prepared remarks, saying, "Surely, my dear friend, I don't have to come here from Illinois to teach Texas manners, do I?"

That scolding met with resounding cheers from the majority in attendance, who had grown exasperated with the interruptions and disturbance. But the demonstrators were undeterred. They shouted even louder. Their noise rose and their anger's intensity grew. A man seated a few rows from the front had to be physically escorted out by police. The man later identified himself as Frank McGehee, a member of the National Indignation Convention.

"I think we need to stay," I said. "It's just too electric in here."

"Look." Jim answered. "My weather comes before your sports, and it's past nine now. Stay as late as you can, and I'll do your sports if I have to!"

About this time police were setting up a rope line from the south stage door through which Stevenson would exit to the limousine waiting for him and his host, Stanley Marcus. As the program neared the end, a crowd of a couple of hundred, some friendly and others not so friendly, had gathered. Police had left the limousine in a decoy position until Stevenson and Marcus were about to emerge, and at the last moment they moved it to within thirty feet of the door.

Suddenly the ambassador emerged, causing a roar from the crowd. Instead of heading straight for the car, he began to shake hands. I turned my camera light on and started filming. I knew intuitively that I needed to keep that camera whirring as long as possible. Then to my amazement, through its tiny eyepiece I saw a woman, grimacing and wild-eyed, appear from the crowd gripping a placard by a wooden handle, swinging it downward over the side of Stevenson's face and ear. I wasn't certain whether the sign had actually struck the ambassador, but I did know that

I had some rather sensational news film. I had already noticed that no other television cameramen were present. All of them apparently had left, since they too were facing their ten o'clock news deadlines. Although I could not hear over the din of the crowd, I was later to learn that Stevenson had asked the woman, "What's the matter, madam? What can I do for you?" to which she had replied, "Well, if you don't know, I can't help you."

As Stevenson hurried to his waiting limousine, a younger group later said to be North Texas State University students continued berating him and, according to witnesses, even spat on him, although I could not tell this through the camera's tiny eyepiece.

It was getting dangerously close to ten o'clock news time. By agreement, Jim had taken the station wagon. I spotted Val Imm, a friend and colleague from the *Dallas Times-Herald,* which owned our station, and I approached her and her date. "Val!" I exclaimed. "I think I got all of that on film! Can you all give me a ride to KRLD-TV?"

"Let's go!" She was as excited as I was, and we both knew it was only twenty minutes to news time. I wanted to alert the station to have the developer solution ready, so we stopped at a pay phone, and I dialed the station, hoping and praying that our photography technician, Henk Dewit, hadn't left for the night. He had not.

"Henk!" I almost shouted, "Get the soup ready! I've got something really hot in my camera!"

"I'll be ready," he replied. Henk Dewit was a Dutch army veteran who'd been imprisoned in a German work camp, and he was always ready.

"And tell Warren Fulks to be ready in the studio at the news desk. I'll only have time to edit the film and write him an outline."

Val, her companion and I sped the five blocks to the television station. As we went, I was unloading the film from the camera, and when we arrived I ran in and handed it to Henk, who put it in the soup. In a few minutes the ten o'clock news was underway.

You never know how a film shot under considerable duress will turn out, but I sat down at my Smith-Corona and made out an outline with the bare facts of what had happened. When the film emerged from the huge developing machine, I took it from Henk and threaded it, still damp, into the little hand-cranked viewer for editing.

"Wow!"

The attacker's contorted face, tongue sticking out, was amazingly clear as the film showed her placard striking Ambassador Stevenson's cheek and ear. Warren Fulks already was well into his newscast, so I didn't have time to make a single edit splice. I rushed the unedited film to the television control room and told the projectionist to put it on the first available projector. Then I ran down the single flight of stairs two steps at a time, raced into the studio, and slipped the barest of outlines to Warren at the news desk.

Wes Wise's film showing the back of Ambassador Adlai Stevenson's head as Cora Fredrickson strikes him with a placard reading "Who Elected You?" The first frame shows the sign as it hits. The second shows the woman, her tongue out and her sign a white blur at lower right after glancing off Stevenson's head. At left talking to Stevenson is the *Dallas Times-Herald's* Val Imm, who sped Wise to KRLD with the film. *Images Courtesy KDFW News*

The professional that he always was, Warren narrated the story dramatically and accurately. He made the rough outline sound finished and polished. He ad-libbed the ending, "A sad night for Dallas."

The next day a frame from the film—a "still," as we called it—was transmitted by Associated Press wirephoto. It appeared in newspapers worldwide. More important to KRLD News, Walter Cronkite's six o'-clock CBS newscast spotlighted the incident, playing the film over and over, using both freeze-frame and slow motion to prove the intent of the demonstrator, a forty-seven-year-old Oak Cliff woman who had claimed, "I was pushed from behind by a Negro." In reality there had been very few blacks at the UN Day observance—and none in the picture.

At the end of his newscast Cronkite praised "our alert young cameraman Wes Wise." It was the only time I remember being called young and alert on national television—or anywhere else.

PROTECTING JFK

Much has been said through the years alleging a lack of security and preparation by the Secret Service, FBI, and the Dallas Police Department before the Kennedy trip to Dallas. By today's standards those criticisms might have merit. But the nation wasn't the same in 1963, and I saw those three agencies hard at work.

About two weeks after the Adlai Stevenson incident, two weeks before the president was to arrive, Eddie Barker called me into his office.

"Wes," he said soberly, "the Secret Service and FBI are intensely interested in the Stevenson film. They want to go over it with you to try and identify people who might be a threat when the president comes."

Some experts in today's journalism ethics would frown on such cooperation between law enforcement and objective reporters. But given the circumstances of the times and the intensity of my experience at the U.N. Day meeting, there was no question in my mind that it was the prudent and proper thing to do.

I was in five or six sessions of two or three hours each that would go something like this: several of us would gather with local and federal officers in the little news department projection room. I would start the film on a 16 mm projector.

"Wait a minute. Let's see that frame again," a Secret Service agent would say.

"Oh, that's old so-and-so," a Dallas police officer would remark. "He might bear watching."

"Start it up again."

"Let me freeze-frame this," I would offer. "That guy in the right background got awfully upset at the U.N. meeting."

The officers took detailed notes. Local police detectives identified certain individuals on the film by name, others by reputation. This we did over and over—repeating, backing up, starting, stopping—as I worked with the law enforcement agencies. I emphasize this cooperation both in the interest of history and to explain my unusual "assignment" later at the Trade Mart, where the president was to speak.

My assignment at that noon luncheon was not an ordinary one. I was an invited guest, along with my wife, Sally, seated at a table on the second balcony. This was strictly social.

When not seated at the table, I wore the official press badge which read, "President Kennedy's Visit to Dallas, November 22, 1963." This was strictly business.

In the social phase of the assignment, I was to watch for anyone I might recognize from the Stevenson incident. I was to advise—unobtrusively, of course—any of the Secret Service or FBI agents if I observed anything even slightly "different," a term I thought those fellows used somewhat self-consciously. By this time, after so many planning sessions, I could easily identify any agent at a glance.

In the business phase I would wear my press identification, first covering the arrival of Air Force One at Love Field along with Frank Glieber. Then I would proceed to a location along the parade route in the median of Lemmon Avenue at Inwood Road, where I would describe the motorcade scene for KRLD radio before Bob Huffaker would take over at Main and Akard downtown.

The arrival at Love Field was joyful and thrilling even to the most hard-bitten of reporters, as the charming first couple met the eager crowd. I ran to the KRLD News station wagon as the president, the first lady, and Nellie and John Connally took their places in the waiting limousine. I drove the mobile unit to my post across from the Cotton Bowling Palace, at Lemmon and Inwood. Soon I was describing the radiant couple on the wagon's two-way microphone. As they passed in the big limousine, I reported, "And I'm sure that everybody in my immediate vicinity would swear they were waving directly at them."

After the presidential parade had passed, I moved on to the Trade Mart for the next part of my assignment. The air of excitement and anticipation was unreal, and the presence of a few protestors on the lawn outside the entrance was surreal. I went inside and met Sally at table 332, where she and I exchanged introductions with other guests.

After a few minutes I sensed some sort of delay. I was thinking, "I feel like some kind of spy trying to be alert for a suspicious action or familiar face while acting socially normal." At this stage of my assignment I wore no press badge.

Across the room, Eddie Barker was broadcasting the proceedings live on the television pool camera's mike. Our table on the second balcony was next to an aisle beside a wall. Beyond the wall were small gift shops. From time to time I noticed some of the FBI and Secret Service agents I'd worked with trying to act inconspicuous while watching every corner.

Suddenly I saw one of them walking briskly down the aisle toward our table. Then came another, trying not to attract attention by running.

"What's going on?" I asked.

I'll never forget his reply: "The worst has happened."

Then I saw for the first time a sign of emotion I would witness many times over the next several days. The normally stoic agent's eyes glistened with tears. I returned to my seat at the table and whispered to Sally what the Secret Service man had said. "You go on home," I said, "Looks like I'm going to be busy."

I began looking for an open shop. I found one and asked for the manager, who had not yet heard what had happened. "President Kennedy has had an accident. May I use your phone to call reports in to KRLD?"

"It's yours as long as you want it," he answered in shock, and for the next hour I filed reports of the scene at the Trade Mart, alternating radio feeds with my colleagues at Parkland, Dealey Plaza, police headquarters, and wherever the developing story led us all.

The personal reactions inside the massive dining area ranged from sheer horror to tearful to heart-wrenching sobs. Two well-dressed matronly women at the next table embraced, crying into each other's shoulders. A young man stood facing a wall, propping his left arm against it and burying his head in his forearm, sobbing uncontrollably. In bizarre contrast, to my shock and dismay, a man at our table continued to stuff a steak into his mouth. I thought, "How can anyone have any kind of an appetite at a time like this?"

In less than an hour, Lee Oswald shot Dallas police officer J. D. Tippit on Tenth Street in Oak Cliff and was captured in the Texas Theater: the prime suspect in the president's assassination.

THE PRESS CONFERENCE THAT MIGHT HAVE CHANGED HISTORY

Weeks earlier, when it had become known that President Kennedy was definitely going to visit Dallas, I wrote him personally and officially on Press Club of Dallas stationery inviting him to hold a news conference under our auspices. Since the avowed purpose of the trip was to mend political fences in Texas in hopes of securing the state's important electoral vote for the Democratic Party, I felt strongly that the president and his advisors would like the publicity and photo opportunities. And—oh, yes—as the club's president, I knew that it would help the club's prestige and recruiting potential.

I suggested that such a conference could be held either before or after the motorcade, at Love Field or at the club's midtown location. Holding that press conference would have entailed arranging the president's scheduled activities, including the Fort Worth breakfast, a half-hour to one hour earlier. I received the following reply on official White House stationery:

> Dear Mr. Wise:
>
> Because I handle the President's appointments and schedule, Mr. Salinger turned over to me your letter of November 8th inviting the President on behalf of the Press Club of Dallas to hold a press conference under their auspices after the luncheon in Dallas on this Friday.
>
> The President is sorry he must have me express his regrets to you. He assures you of his thanks for your thoughtfulness of him, nonetheless, and sends you and all those of the Press Club of Dallas his best wishes.
>
> Sincerely,
> Kenneth O'Donnell
> Special Assistant to the President

The direction of history has often been changed by a difference of hours, minutes, even seconds. If President Kennedy's timetable had been altered for a press conference, if his motorcade had passed the School Book Depository minutes earlier or later, the assassin might not have been able to hide unnoticed on the dingy floor at that fateful window.

THE PRESS HITS DALLAS

Press and broadcast coverage influenced both local and national reaction to President Kennedy's assassination and the city where it took place. The media and public sentiment both inside and outside Dallas are intertwined both literally and psychologically.

For years before 1963, the so-called Dallas Oligarchy had been the subject of numerous articles in both local and national press. The city had been politically controlled by a small group of mostly wealthy businessmen who were often unjustly criticized as selfish and greedy. In truth most of them were passionate citizens who contributed time and resources for the good of the city. Few associated themselves with the far right wing.

These civic leaders did, however, jealously guard their control of the community's political and civic life even though many of them did not live inside the Dallas city limits. Since most of them were either conservative Democrats—common in Texas then—or Republicans, it is easy to see why the press came into Dallas with preconceptions of the city and its reaction to the arrival of a liberal Democratic president.

The Press Club of Dallas was quite active in those days, both socially and visually. The purple and orange décor of its headquarters was hardly inspirational, but the spirit, location and lively conversation of the place most assuredly were. Located in the middle of the busiest part of downtown Dallas halfway between Jack Ruby's Carousel Club and the original Neiman-Marcus on Commerce Street, it was a place for members of the media to hang out together. I was especially pleased that the print media, by electing me the club's president, were at last accepting one of those weird show-biz electronics guys as their leader.

Between assignments the day after the president was assassinated, I called the club manager, Martha Trenary. "Martha, we've got to stay open over the weekend as late as possible and try to assist all these press people from out of town."

Martha was way ahead of me. "I've arranged for some typewriters and office space down the hall as well as here in the club," she said, "and they've already gotten the word that this is the place to be."

"Okay, good. But Martha," I said, "we've got to be careful not to look like a bunch of public relations people shilling for the city. Let's just be friendly and helpful and give them a nice place to gather if they want."

It soon became apparent that this task would be difficult at best. Visiting reporters' preconceived notions about the city became obvious even in casual conversations. We were seeing the out-of-town press in the most informal of circumstances, with its hair down, not for print. Many of the bull sessions for which press clubs anywhere are noted became heated arguments. *Dallas Times-Herald* writer Dick Hitt, during a discussion at the bar, exchanged blows with a member of the foreign press.

In their efforts to accommodate fellow journalists from out of town, writers and photographers from both the *Dallas Morning News* and the *Dallas Times-Herald* discovered that some of their guests had rifled their files and stolen valuable photographs.

On the radio-television side, some of the CBS people, often without even introducing themselves, invaded the KRLD newsroom and tried to take over our desks. One network producer had stationed himself at the desk of our assistant news director, Jim Underwood. Bad move. Underwood, who had already experienced some problems with the visitors, walked in from an assignment and found the CBS man leaning back in Jim's chair, feet on his desk, talking on Jim's telephone.

"Who the hell do you think you are?" Underwood shouted. Action in the newsroom stopped cold. The guy looked totally stunned as we watched in delight.

"I don't put my feet on the furniture in my own home, much less in this office, and I don't expect you to."

The fellow bounced forward, righting himself as Jim, with an umpire's motion toward the door, commanded, "Out!"

The fellow later became one of CBS's top producers.

The three-day media drama seemed to bring out both the creative best and the personal, even prejudiced, worst in journalists. The visiting press, national and international, called us "redneck Texans" and "gun-happy cowboys." We called them "carpetbagger Yankees" and "ill-mannered snobs." These were, of course, among the kinder terms. But believe it or not, amidst all of this adversarial rhetoric, a certain camaraderie began to develop in late-night discussions in the press club. Along with the heated arguments there were solid, sensible discussions.

The out-of-town press invariably wanted to explore our minds about this mysterious Dallas "oligarchy." Many of them assumed that the city leaders were synonymous with the John Birch Society, General Edwin Walker and the National Indignation bunch. When we would try to explain that Dallas civic figures wouldn't consider even the remotest association with those groups or individuals, the out-of-towners' retort would be, "Then why hasn't the city gotten rid of them?"

Amazingly, that question seemed always to come from the mouths of the staunchest First Amendment rights advocates.

WAITING FOR OSWALD

By Sunday all of us knew too well that we were in the middle of what would probably be the biggest story of our careers. So it was especially significant to me when News Director Eddie Barker called me into his office that morning.

"Dan Rather was scheduled to cover Oswald's arrival at the county," he said, "but he's involved in CBS negotiations for an amateur film of the shooting [the Abraham Zapruder film, I would learn later] so you'll cover the arrival."

The entrance to the jail building on Houston Street was in sight of the already-infamous sixth-floor window.

When I arrived at the corner of Houston and Elm, our custom TV bus, "The Blue Goose," was already set up there, and an area across the street from the jail building had been roped off for a crowd of several hundred lined up along the curb.

I walked the area and noticed a grate about five feet square in the sidewalk next to the jail building. I remember thinking to myself, "I wonder if the underground beneath that grate has been inspected?"

The veteran sheriff, Bill Decker, soon appeared on the scene in his familiar gray suit and fedora hat. "Are you ready, Sheriff?" I inquired half-joking.

"We're always ready," he replied.

Although we reporters were unsure of the exact time of the transfer,

I suspected the sheriff was present to supervise the arrival any minute. A member of the television crew handed me a mike and pointed to the location of the camera atop the bus.

This was my big moment on national television with the whole world watching on their Sunday off. I was nervous, the adrenaline surging, but I was ready.

"Something's happened!" someone shouted from The Blue Goose. "Stand by!"

As often happens at a time like this, the reporter on the scene knows less than the crew behind the scene. Slowly, agonizingly, it trickled down to me that Oswald had been seriously wounded in the basement of the city jail.

Sheriff Decker walked out and confirmed the startling news. The crowd, observing the confusion on the street, could not comprehend.

"We don't know yet who did it," the sheriff mumbled. "I guess I better tell these people." He walked into the middle of the street and faced the crowd, now three or four deep along the curb. Then came one of the most memorable of all my experiences of that unbelievable weekend.

Outside the Dallas County Jail, Sheriff Bill Decker tells reporters that Oswald has been shot and will not arrive. *Photograph courtesy The Sixth Floor Museum at Dealey Plaza. Photographer Andy Hanson,* Dallas Times Herald *Collection*

Spectators outside the county jail cheer at the news that Oswald has been shot. *Photograph courtesy The Sixth Floor Museum at Dealey Plaza. Photographer Andy Hanson,* Dallas Times Herald *Collection*

"Ladies and gentlemen," the sheriff announced, "Lee Harvey Oswald has been shot and is on his way to Parkland Hospital."

Like an explosion, a blood-curdling cheer and resounding applause erupted from the crowd. All the pent-up emotions of Dallas, Texas, seemed to emerge at that moment: hurt, confusion, fear, disgust and, most of all, indescribable sadness and sorrow for a fallen president, for his lovely wife and two beautiful children. I stood there in the middle of the street, dead microphone in hand, shaking my head.

RUBY AND I

The day after the assassination, Saturday, Eddie Barker had called me into his office. "I want you to take your camera," he said, "and try to trace Oswald's route as close as you can."

I drove one of our Pontiac Catalina wagons with KRLD News lettered on its side along with the CBS eye. My first stop, the already infamous Texas School Book Depository, was only a few blocks away. I angled the shiny mobile unit into the curb across from the building on what is now the extension of Houston Street. At the time it was not a through street, serving as a drive toward the railroad tracks at the rear of the building. I picked up the two-way radio microphone, made contact with the base station and gave a brief radio report on the scene there.

The "grassy knoll," as early reports had christened it for all time, was already covered with every variety of flowers as well as cards and letters honoring the fallen president. Moving among those flowers and mourners, my colleague Bill Mercer did a memorable piece that day, reading cards on the wreaths and interviewing Dallasites there to pay their respects. Near the gathering banks of flowers, I finished my radio dispatch, placed the mike back in its cradle, and like so many Dallas citizens at those moments, sat in deep reflection.

"Hey, Wes!"

The voice came from the direction of the railroad tracks at the rear of the building. I turned to see the portly figure of a man in a dark suit, half-waddling, half-trotting, as he came toward me. He was wearing a fedora-style hat which would later become familiar and famous.

"Oh, my goodness," I thought. "This is all I need right now—to stop and take time to talk to Jack Ruby."

Ruby was the ultimate news reporter groupie of his day. Invariably he would show up at sports events, major automobile accidents, even many funerals and weddings. He was truly a news-hound man-about-town. True to form, he had been at police headquarters the night before when Bill Mercer crouched below the accused assassin, whom police had brought out for the media to see. Jack Ruby was maintaining his reputation for being where the action was.

He leaned into my driver's-side window. "Isn't this awful? Where were you when it happened?" he asked.

"I was at the Trade Mart," I said. Then I remarked that I had taken film of the western saddles that were to have been gifts from the City of Dallas to the Kennedy children, Caroline and John-John. Tears welled up in Ruby's eyes.

"I just hope they don't make Jackie come to Dallas for the trial," he said. His voice broke as he added, "That would be terrible for that little lady."

I excused myself and drove on to film Lee Harvey Oswald's rooming house. Reflecting on that conversation, I have wondered whether Ruby was hoping that I might do a radio interview with him. Such a thing would have been a historic part of that sad weekend's coverage. But at the time, my only thought was to get away from Ruby and continue on my assignment: covering the Oswald stops.

I thought it odd that Ruby had approached the news wagon from the direction of the railroad tracks at the rear of the building, since the crowd was gathered principally at the front.

Across Dealey Plaza the next morning, I was waiting for Oswald's arrival at the county jail when Jack Ruby killed him before police could transfer him there.

Like it or not, I was stuck with some special relationship that Ruby had concocted between us, and Eddie Barker assigned me to cover practically every minute of his trial. I was subpoenaed as a witness by both District Attorney Henry Wade and Ruby's defense team, headed by Melvin Belli. The prosecution wanted to show that Ruby was taking an unusual interest in the site the day following the assassination. The defense wanted to show his emotional reaction. *Life* magazine described my testimony:

> Mr. Wes Wise of TV station KRLD said that Ruby was in tears when they were talking about the two western saddles that were to have been given by the city as a present to the Kennedy children.
>
> Assistant District Attorney William Alexander: "Was he excited?"
>
> Wise: "Touched."
>
> Mr. Joe Tonahill for the defense (trying to sew it up): "He broke down and cried?"
>
> Wise: "I would not describe it as breaking down and crying—I'd say there were tears in his eyes."

A JAILBREAK AND A NOTE FROM RUBY

I was assigned to cover at least some part of the Ruby trial every day it was in session—largely, I assumed, because I'd covered the Adlai Stevenson incident, then had been confronted by Jack Ruby at the School Book Depository the day following the assassination. Several aspects of the trial involved me personally. Several witnesses testified that Ruby tried to contact me "on the pay phone at the garage next to the Carousel Club" after our chance meeting at the depository building the day after the assassination. I naturally wondered what the purpose of the call might have been.

Probably the most remarkable sidebar of the trial had nothing to do with the trial itself. It happened by surprise on Friday, March 6, two days after I'd been on the stand for the prosecution. After a short recess called by Judge Brown, I was casually walking down the hall just outside the courtroom when I saw a woman employee of the Dallas County sheriff's office, whom I knew slightly, walking toward me with a terrified expression on her face. Next to her was a young man thrusting an apparent gun into her ribs.

"Look out, Wes!" she shouted. "He's got a gun!"

They were headed straight toward the Brown courtroom where the Ruby trial was taking place.

"My God," I thought. "He's going in there to shoot Jack!"

But I turned to see him walk right past a line of spectators along the short stairway waiting their turn to attend the trial. They merely turned and watched in disbelief.

The inmate from the county jail on the top floors of the building had shaped a fake pistol from a bar of soap, blackened it with shoe polish, and somehow seized the deputy, Ruth Thornton, as a hostage. He made his way onto Main Street but was quickly apprehended by police with no resistance.

The press had been told early in the trial not to attempt to interview Ruby. But nobody said anything about notes. So I handed a note with a series of questions to Joe Tonahill, one of Ruby's attorneys, to be given to Ruby after final testimony and before Judge Brown's charge to the jury.

I purposely made the questions somewhat innocuous, thinking they would neither be given to Ruby nor answered by him any other way. So I was frankly surprised when the results made the front-page top fold of the *Dallas Times-Herald*.

RUBY FEELS "CONFUSED"

Newsman Wes Wise of KRLD-AM-FM-TV, the *Times-Herald* stations, got an exclusive sampling of Jack Ruby's feelings Friday as the murder trial neared the jury stages.

Wise submitted in writing four questions to Ruby, who in turn answered them in writing.

The questions were:

"How do you feel?"

Ruby replied: "Confused."

"Are you hopeful?"

Ruby wrote: "Yes."

"Do you think you will be acquitted?"

Ruby wrote: "Yes."

"Would you like to testify?"

And Ruby wrote: "Yes, but Mr. Belli knows better, I guess."

JACK'S DREAM

If Jack Ruby had lived and been freed from prison, Dallas might have been different, and it might not have been a pretty sight. Ruby's attorney Joe Tonahill, who felt that his client's eventual freedom was always a distinct possibility, discussed with me what might have been, shortly before his death in his hometown of Jasper.

"There's just no telling what Jack could have done," Tonahill told me, "With his promotional and marketing skills the sky could've been the limit."

Although Tonahill did not come right out and say it, anyone who ever attended Ruby's clubs would agree that there might have been very little in good taste displayed. Rather than the sky as the limit, the gutter might have been more likely.

Ruby would have been within his rights to make the most of his historic notoriety in his nightclub, and he was the sort of self-promoter to do it. Renaming the Carousel Club, Ruby might have lined the walls of his establishment with photo blowups of the assassination of the president and the Oswald shooting. The curious would have been attracted by the famous club as well as its unpredictable owner-proprietor-master of ceremonies.

Members of the media have speculated that Jack might even have hired himself out for five-minute individual interviews. He would have basked in the attention, and many assassination buffs would gladly pay for such an experience. The original admission price would be whatever the market would bear, and up from there. Of course this would have been devastating to the citizens of Dallas, who would have to absorb another worldwide blow. The City Fathers might have objected, but nobody would have known better than Jack Ruby that such a public outcry would flood the media and thus benefit his promotions in the end.

THE TEXAS SCHOOL BOOK DEPOSITORY

After 1970 the Texas School Book Depository building stood empty for twelve years under two different ownerships, and there were persistent rumblings that it should be demolished. Even a decade after the assassination, while I was serving as mayor of Dallas, a member of the city council, Fred Zeder, led a determined effort to have the building torn down. He won considerable support from members of the Republican Party, of which he was a longtime supporter.

"We need to do away with this terrible blight on the city," said Zeder, and he succeeded in creating a behind-the-scenes groundswell of public opinion for that viewpoint.

My response: "This is a historic building, however infamous, and it must be preserved for history."

In addition, assassination conspiracy buffs were already numbered in the thousands, and I could see the destruction of the building as a ripe opportunity for them to shout "coverup," and in one sense they would be right. Rather than simply doing away with a civic blight, Dallas would surely be accused of doing away with invaluable evidence for future investigators and historians. Even John Connally once told me, "You've got to save it."

At the peak of the public outcry a decade later, a Dallas City Council meeting was scheduled. A resolution was to be proposed endorsing taking down the building. Ironically, it was two members of the political arm of the Dallas oligarchy, the Citizens Charter Association, who first came to me with detailed information of the plan. It was an eleven-member city council back then, and I did some hard lobbying to round up support to defeat the resolution. I knew that I had six, maybe even seven, votes. But I also knew that all ten members of the council either were, or had been, members of the Citizens Charter Association, whose candidate for mayor I had soundly defeated. Political pressure could change those minds in a heartbeat.

The council chambers were buzzing with rumors when councilwoman Anita Martinez asked to be recognized and, according to plan, started into a proposed resolution to do away with the building. I interrupted, tapping my gavel, lightly but politely, on the council desk.

"That resolution is out of order," I said, mustering my strongest announcer's voice. "The City of Dallas has no jurisdiction and no authority whatsoever over that building. Next order of business."

Thank goodness, that was the end of that. The County of Dallas did a magnificent job of remodeling the structure into its administration building, which now also houses The Sixth Floor Museum at Dealey Plaza.

THE CITY THAT KILLED THE PRESIDENT

For years Dallas citizens experienced verbal slams at their city, although such slurs have become much less numerous in recent years. The emergence of the professional football Dallas Cowboys as "America's Team" and the popularity of the television series *Dallas,* especially overseas, helped improve the city's image dramatically. However, my personal worst experience came a full decade after the awful event, on the occasion of the 1973 meeting of the U.S. Conference of Mayors.

There is always considerable press coverage of these annual meetings both nationally and locally by reporters from the individual cities. This particular year I had received more media attention than usual for two reasons. First, we were closing in on the tenth anniversary of the assassination. Second, I had just been reelected against the political organization that the press identified as the "oligarchy."

A group of seven or eight of us were standing around during the cocktail hour sipping our drinks and engaged in friendly conversation about issues of the conference. Suddenly, during a lull in the conversation, the mayor of a medium-sized midwestern city blurted out, "How does it feel to be the mayor of the city that killed the president?"

A stunned silence fell over the group, and for a fleeting moment I thought of striking back physically. The media was already doing "Ten Years Later" stories with me, and as a journalist myself I knew that any kind of a scene would be reported nationally as well as locally back to both our cities. It wasn't easy, but I stood silent, glowering at the man.

Later in the evening, one by one, the individuals in the gathering came over to me. Maybe they discerned the hurt I felt for the city I loved just as they loved theirs.

"It could have happened to any one of us," said one.

"That was a low blow, and we all feel bad about it," said another.

The next morning at the coffee hour, the mayor who made the remark approached me somewhat hesitantly. "Look, I guess the liquor was talking last night," he said, "and I'd just like to apologize. I've been catching hell from my colleagues, and rightfully so."

I accepted his apology. We smiled and shook hands.

8

The Trials of Jacob Rubenstein

BOB HUFFAKER

"I'M JACK RUBY. YOU ALL KNOW ME!"

Before Parkland doctors had pronounced Oswald dead, a few local lawyers showed up to try to bail Jack Ruby out on an assault charge, but Tom Howard was the only one left to represent him when the charge evolved into murder. Howard, a veteran criminal defense attorney, was a friend of Ruby's family. Jack's business partner Ralph Paul had called him, and despite his low-budget operation from a storefront office with neither secretary nor law library, Tom Howard had defended clients in twenty-five capital cases without one defendant getting the death penalty. He had represented pimps, whores, and junkies, but he was very good at his job. And he looked like Harry Truman, even to his hat.

Howard was preparing a defense of murder without malice, which would have carried a sentence of no more than five years. But Ruby's family thought that the case deserved a better-known attorney. There was talk of hiring Charles Tessmer of Dallas or Percy Foreman of Houston, Texas's two high-profile criminal defense attorneys. But before long, Ruby's family brought in a far-fetched specialist in tort law.

A California friend steered them to the flamboyant, self-promoting San Francisco plaintiff's lawyer Melvin Belli, who presided over a California coterie and fired a cannon from his building's rooftop to celebrate each victory. The charismatic counselor arrived in Dallas already in character as the crusading intellectual who would triumph over backward Texas injustice. He mounted the stage to battle Henry Wade,

Reporters question Ruby's attorney Tom Howard at police headquarters after his client has shot Oswald. *Photograph courtesy The Sixth Floor Museum at Dealey Plaza.* Dallas Times Herald *Collection*

the Dallas DA, who had earned a reputation winning capital cases. Wade, later defendant in Roe vs. Wade, was relentless in pushing for the death penalty. He was a perfect foil for Belli's role as a civil-rights advocate.

"My name is Melvin Bell-eye," the Californian told me when I picked up the newsroom phone. He had heard my newscast announcing his arrival as Ruby's defense chief. I had pronounced it *belly*, which indeed proved to be one of his prominent features.

"My apologies," I said.

"Bell-eye," he said.

"Mr. Belli, can you tell me anything about whether you'll go for a change of venue?"

"Not at this time. But remember, it's Bell-eye."

"Got it. Like *casus belli*. Thanks for letting me know."

Belli, the self-proclaimed "King of Torts," loved the spotlight and prided himself in representing Hollywood's beautiful people, but clients had trouble getting between him and the media's nearest camera. His horn-rimmed glasses were owlish, and a leonine mane of graying hair swept his brow in meticulous disarray. He drove a Rolls and dressed in scarlet-lined cloaks—the soul of charm and one of the nation's most famous lawyers, but personal injury was his field, not capital murder.

Melvin Belli came to Dallas apparently determined that defending the vigilante avenger would make him a Clarence Darrow in the bereaved nation's eyes. When he entered the case on December 10, we covered his press conference in Dallas. Our first questions concerned the possibility of a venue change, but he downplayed the likelihood that he would try to move the trial elsewhere, stating that he thought the locals could be fair and that they'd seen no more television than the rest of the nation. But on Friday the 13th in New York, he said that he would press for a change of venue. In the eyes of the nation, Dallas was looking like a hotbed of hatred, and it wouldn't be long before Belli had decided to put the entire city on trial in a push for a not-guilty verdict.

Meanwhile in the county jail, his client got weirder by the day, wondering where his dream had gone askew. Jack had always wanted to be accepted as an insider—admired as a generous guy who could get rough with the likes of, well, strippers and rowdy drunks too dazed to resist. He had failed to envision actually being charged with murder for what he had conceived as an act of patriotism. Ruby had fancied himself a hero, and he was deflated when the King of Torts hired specialists to sully his righteousness with hints of mental problems. Now that Jack Ruby was suddenly confined, and deprived of the Preludin and Benzedrine that he had come to know so well, his mental state began to decline.

Melvin Belli cultivated expert witnesses with titles and opinions. As Dallas' D.A. Henry Wade prepared to prosecute Jack for Lee Oswald's murder, Belli would build a defense on the arcane issue of Ruby's supposed psychomotor epilepsy. Jack Ruby was uneasy with such questions about his mental competence. He'd never been known for his intellect, but questions about his sanity insulted his sense of importance.

Wes Wise and Pat Dean were to be witnesses as the prosecution built its case for premeditation, and Wes would be subpoenaed by the defense, too.

Sheriff Bill Decker made sure that we wore bright orange press passes with our photos in black-and-white. He was determined to control reporters rather than have them dominate his territory as they had Chief Curry's. Crafty and tough in his mid-sixties, Decker was king of his domain, and he presided daily over a court of deputies and reporters in his office. We liked and respected him, and he was cordial enough to remember our names.

Even seated at his desk, Bill Decker wore his snap-brim fedora and business suit. He was medium sized, slung low and powerful. Black-rimmed glasses framed his narrow eyes, each of which was slightly independent of the other. Decker was a skeptic packing heat under his coat, and I never heard him raise his gravelly voice.

The sheriff wasn't taking any chances with security when Ruby made his first appearance in court. Two days before Christmas, he had his men on hand in force at the bail hearing. Plainclothes deputies lined hallways and courtroom walls. Several sat behind Ruby, facing the crowd and scanning the courtroom. Reporters gained admission only with credentials, and we wore our press badges. In secret, deputies held Ruby in an adjoining room for hours before they brought him in.

Texas was the only state besides Colorado that permitted trial judges to decide whether courtroom proceedings would be televised, and Judge Joe B. Brown, a former peace justice and county court judge before winning election as a state district judge, loved publicity. He sucked on a pipe, joked with reporters, and was known for running an informal court with plenty of press access.

VIEWERS, TELEVISION, AND THE COURT

The networks had asked to televise the trial live. But Brown had hired Sam Bloom, head of a Dallas advertising firm, as his press advisor, and Bloom joined prosecutors in dissuading him from permitting cameras in court. The beautifully wrinkled old grandstander, probably as sorry as Melvin Belli to lose the cameras, prohibited them—live television, film or still ones, as well as sound recorders—when court was in session.

Brown's order restricted our equipment to hallways, but Sam Bloom assigned reporters seats in court and settled squabbling over them by moving proceedings into a larger courtroom. Because of that special arrangement, the defense later moved for a mistrial even before testimony started, on grounds that reserving most seats for the press excluded the general citizenry, denying Ruby's right to a public trial.

This trial was unique in several ways, the most obvious one being that the nation had seen the crime on television. History held no judicial precedent for such a public murder, and while I'd been broadcasting it live, my uncertainty about legal consequences had kept me from pressing Pat Dean for Ruby's name. As a journalist, I was being overcautious, although I did grill Pat hard enough to make an old police friend call me from Boston to bitch me out for it. In those moments after Ruby shot Oswald, Pat Dean and I had been friends in uncharted territory on national television, and I wasn't going to endanger his career by probing him for Ruby's name.

Caution had been in order, though. The defense would later attempt to disqualify jurors who had seen the murder on television, under the legal exclusion of witnesses from a jury. To counter that argument, the prosecution successfully distinguished between those who had witnessed the televised crime and those who might actually be called as witnesses in the case.

Another unique quality of the case was the way that television would affect the issue of whether the trial should be moved out of Dallas. Soon after the bail hearing, which Tom Howard had initiated, would come the defense motion for a change of venue. But since most people everywhere across the land had seen the murder live or replayed, the argument for relocating the trial to any other city lost much of its logic and force.

THE DEFENSE USES THE MEDIA

But a motion for a venue change is one more trap laid for a trial's appellate phase, and Belli would move for one—not on grounds that too many Dallasites had seen the murder, but instead that their waspish city harbored a generalized tendency to prejudices, including anti-Semitism. He and his friend Joe Tonahill, a huge, rich, drawling lawyer from Jasper, in the East Texas piney woods, began to talk *real ugly* about Dallas as they postured for the media. The two flamboyant defenders were loud, witty and articulate, but their conduct in court was so unruly that Henry Wade's prosecution team feared it might provide later grounds for appealing the conviction he sought. Tom Howard's inevitable departure from the case would leave the young and able Dallas lawyer Phil Burleson as the only properly behaving man at the defense table. Concerned over a possible appeal based upon inadequate defense counsel, Wade and his assistant counsel Bill Alexander also were prepared to call for a pause in testimony unless at least one attorney licensed in Texas was present—a situation that never occurred, however, throughout the trial. Phil Burleson was the defense's man who booked the proceedings and kept track of Judge Brown's rulings on objections, motions, evidentiary questions and the like, but he was a silent partner among noisy ones.

COVERING BAIL HEARINGS

At the December bail hearing, as at the change-of-venue hearing and later the trial, we were allowed film cameras only in hallways, and there would be no live telecasts until, as it turned out, the following March on the day of the verdict. Henry Wade laid his case by calling Captain Will Fritz and Detective Jim Leavelle as eyewitnesses, and on cross-examination, Melvin Belli foreshadowed his strategy when he asked both officers whether their security on November 24 had been extensive out of fear that someone with "an inflamed mind" might try to kill Oswald.

To establish Ruby's movements before he shot Oswald, the defense called Little Lynn to appear at the bail hearing, and she showed up great with child and giggling like the teenager she was. The Western Union clerk who'd time-stamped her telegraphed rent money also took the stand, as did Ruby's roommate George Senator, whose living arrangement suggested the unspoken question of homosexuality as assistant prosecutor Bill Alexander cross-examined him. The judge denied bail temporarily, allowing for another bail hearing to follow, and Brown joined Belli and Tonahill in lighthearted hallway appearances before a crowd of reporters.

At the next bail hearing, a disorderly affair on the twentieth of January, the genial judge and defense continued their hallway press appearances, and Belli continued to tip his hand to the prosecution as he called psychiatric witnesses. He was so intemperate that the hearing was barely within the judge's control. Some of the local reporters were quietly calling Brown "Judge Joe B. Buffoon" behind his back.

Melvin Belli lost no opportunity to insult the prosecution, but assistant D.A. Bill Alexander gave as good as he got. Alexander, a pale ectomorph with acne scars and a sadistic glint in fiercely cold eyes, was himself a skilled and relentless needler. Having anticipated prosecuting

Oswald, he'd joked to reporters after the assassin's death that you "can't have rabbit stew without a rabbit." During the hearing, he clashed with Belli as he questioned a Jewish psychiatrist about Jews talking with their hands. When Belli insistently mispronounced the name of Wade's assistant Jim Bowie as "Mr. Boy," the prosecution jabbed back by calling him "Mr. Belly," as I'd done earlier in innocence.

VALENTINE'S DAY MASSACRE

Brown agreed to the defense requests for neurological tests, and Belli withdrew his bail motion to pursue a change of venue, which Brown temporarily denied at a hearing on Valentine's Day—while a little massacre began among the defense team and client.

Before Belli arrived, Tom Howard had been pursuing the smartest strategy: get Ruby off with five years on murder without malice by proving that the act had been impulsive, a sudden outburst of anger from an otherwise sane person. That time-stamped Western Union receipt almost certainly would prove that Ruby had killed Oswald within four minutes of wiring Little Lynn's twenty-five dollars, strongly contradicting any claim that he'd been planning the fatal attack. He might have harbored murderous thoughts about Oswald as many other Americans did, but fantasizing about killing the bastard didn't constitute actually planning to murder him. Tom Howard had a solid case for murder without malice. In a flash of rage, Ruby had shot a handcuffed and defenseless person much as he had beaten only smaller men, drunks, and the occasional stripper who'd triggered his explosive temper. And true to the pattern of his other eruptions, he'd staged this one in front of a crowd.

Not only had Tom Howard begun preparing a strategy for a light sentence; he'd also wanted to handle the case quietly. In contrast, Belli insisted upon being the star. He wanted to walk Ruby out in triumph scot-free, and he was willing to risk his client's life to pull that off. He never gave the Dallas lawyer's strategy a second glance, and the two broke up on Valentine's Day.

As expected, Tom Howard, pushed aside in planning and proceedings, resigned from the case. And Ruby and his family, appalled at Belli's flagrant courtroom behavior and his preening before the press, infuriated Belli with a tentative move to approach Dallas attorney Charles

Tessmer, one of the state's sharpest criminal defense lawyers, as well-known then as Houston's Percy Foreman. Belli got wind of the overture and refused to allow such a thing, angrily confronting Ruby about it in the courtroom as jury selection was about to begin on Monday the 17th.

VIEWERS AS WITNESSES

The judge would reserve his change-of-venue ruling until jury selection had proven either successful or not, and Belli continued with the apparent strategy of trying to make the process fail miserably. When jury selection started, he began a transparent—and ultimately unproductive—effort to prolong and confuse the process. He raised the obstacle of disqualifying "witnesses" who had seen the murder on TV, and having failed at that maneuver, he used up more than three hours shouting questions before finally rejecting the first prospective panelist. He continued badgering the next prospects, insulting Dallas, and using up his peremptory challenges—hoping, it seemed, to make such a shambles of the selection phase that the judge would be compelled to acquiesce in moving the trial out of Dallas.

But Judge Brown wanted the limelight himself and wasn't going to do that. Meanwhile, the King of Torts' aggressive posturing was wasting peremptory challenges and previewing his tactics before the prosecution. Apparently confident that he would win the venue change, Belli persisted in his confrontational anti-Dallas tactics for several days. Our broadcast from the police basement entered the picture again when he tried without success to subpoena one prospective juror as a witness, thus reviving the question of excluding TV witnesses as jurors.

Belli snapped at prospective jurors and ridiculed them as typifying a city of hatred and bigotry. But as more were seated, Belli began to sense that his chances for a venue change were getting slimmer, and his examination of likely-looking prospects became downright cordial.

After fourteen days of examining more than 150 prospects, Belli and Wade seated their last two jurors on March 3, when Brown was ailing and Judge J. Frank Wilson presided in his place. Wilson was a strict jurist, and proceedings moved smoother and faster that day, both sides moderating their behavior before a judge who brooked no hijinks. After press accounts remarked that Wilson had brought decorum to the day's proceedings, Brown returned the next day temporarily infused with dignity. Brown opened the case by denying the handful of defense motions, including venue change, and both prosecution and defense became more circumspect before the seated jury.

REPORTERS INSIDE AND OUTSIDE THE COURTROOM

Inside the courtroom, Frank Glieber and Wes Wise took notes in our assigned KRLD News seat, and I sat in on sessions when they were elsewhere—and when Wes's duties as a subpoenaed witness kept him out of a session. In the hallways, we covered impromptu bull sessions with Belli, Ruby, Tonahill, and Brown.

As Ruby came and went between sessions, I eventually developed a routine of walking briskly beside him with the mike while George Phenix, Sandy Sanderson, or Dan Garza danced backward ahead of us like Ginger Rogers, filming us with a big shoulder-mounted sound camera. I didn't ask questions that might compromise the defendant's rights, and Ruby was so garrulous and eager to talk that I needed only to get him started. Knowing that this groupie was especially fascinated with Wes, all I had to do was drop Wes's name along with KRLD's, and Ruby was off and talking. Once he said, "I didn't see you yesterday. Where were you?"

"Well I'm off duty some days, Jack," I told him as we marched down the hallway, the dance troupe of reporters backing along with hot portable lights.

Wes took the stand on the trial's opening morning, as the prosecution laid its foundation for premeditation. Ruby had buttonholed Wes at the School Book Depository, across from the county jail, the day before he shot Oswald. The prosecution wanted to show that the defendant was lurking where Oswald was to have been transferred—maybe stalking the assassin, waiting for his arrival from Curry's jail to Decker's.

Wes had more different roles in the case than any of us. Not only had the defendant accosted him the day before the crime, but the next day Wes was waiting at the county jail for the Oswald arrival that never happened. A quick prosecution objection stopped his answer when big Joe Tonahill asked him in cross-examination whether the crowd there had cheered to hear of the Oswald shooting. Belli would try to prove that

Ruby was epileptic, and Tonahill, who blared about Ruby's "shootin' that Communist," was trying to make him a heroic epileptic.

RES GESTAE AND PHENIX'S FILM

As prosecution testimony continued over the next few days, Melvin Belli cross-examined police who testified about Ruby's saying, "I hope I killed the son of a bitch," "I intended to shoot him three times," and "I did it because you couldn't." The San Franciscan brought up the officers' reports and insinuated that their writing might contradict their oral testimony. Henry Wade countered by offering to enter the reports in evidence, a breach of judicial procedure that nonetheless foiled Belli's strategy. Both sides knew that Brown couldn't admit written statements by a witness on the stand, but Wade's act was squelching Belli's crafty hints that officers' unnamed reports might cast doubt on their testimony. Belli had painted himself into a corner, and he found himself having to object to Wade's wiley willingness to allow written statements of a witness into evidence.

On the third day of testimony, George Phenix's film of the murder became a center of attention. Lieutenant Jack Revill, who had followed me all the way to Fort Hood, pointed out what the film showed, identifying reporters and police as its frames showed Ruby advancing toward Oswald from beside where George and I had stood. Not only was the film solid evidence, but showing it to the jury also weakened any future claim that TV witnesses couldn't serve as jurors, since now they'd seen at least one television version of it in court.

The final prosecution witness was Sergeant Patrick Trevore Dean, whose testimony was Wade's strongest support for premeditation. Having finished talking to Tom Pettit and me on live television, Pat had gone directly up into the jail, joined on the way by Secret Service chief Forrest Sorrels, and both men had questioned Ruby, stripped to his shorts and ready to talk. The timing of Pat's conversation with Ruby was a critical issue, since he testified that it had taken place some ten minutes after Ruby had pulled the trigger. The defendant's other immediate statements had been admitted under the *res gestae* provision, which allows such statements as evidence only if they are part of the crime itself or a spontaneous utterance in the immediate spirit of the crime. Belli objected to Pat's testifying about what Ruby had told him in jail, but the attorney had already weakened the *res gestae* argument by bringing up other things that Ruby had told police hours after he'd talked to Pat, including reminding them to rescue Sheba the dachshund, still outside in his parked car.

Over Belli's strident demands for an immediate mistrial, Pat testified that Ruby had told him he'd walked down the Main Street ramp as Lieutenant Rio "Sam" Pierce drove out, that he'd wanted to spare Kennedy's widow a trial, that he'd hoped to prove "Jews do have guts," and, most damaging, that he'd first thought of killing Oswald when he'd seen him in the press showing the midnight after the assassination. Belli, with a technique he'd long used at the slightest suggestion of Dallas bigotry, made Pat repeat the Semitic reference: "Jews. J-E-W-S, was it, officer?"

In cross-examination, Belli again resurrected the question of a witness's written report, prohibited as evidence under Texas law. When he asked Pat whether he'd submitted one, the sergeant said, of course, that he had. When Belli asked to see the report, Pat took it out and handed it to him, repocketing his security-investigation report, which he'd taken out and unfolded with the first sheet of paper. Belli repeated his earlier mistake, making such an issue of the remaining report that Henry Wade magnanimously offered to enter both reports in evidence, sending the infuriated Belli into a dither of objections that became uncharacteristically inarticulate. Pat's testimony had nailed the argument for premeditation, and Henry Wade rested his case.

THE STRIPPER AND THE JAILBREAK

Poor pregnant Karen Carlin was to be the first defense witness, as Belli hoped to dispel any suspicion that her time-stamped telegram had been some advance ploy to hide Ruby's intentions. The nineteen-year-old stripper would've been as unlikely a collaborator in such a deception as Ruby would have been in a conspiracy. "Little Lynn" was anything but little now, her delivery already overdue, and she suddenly found herself in the middle of a jailbreak.

Four floors above the courtroom in the Dallas County Jail, several prisoners had escaped their cells after one of them had carved a convincing pistol from a cake of soap and blacked it with shoe polish. Sheriff Bill Decker and his deputies dampened and subdued most would-be escapees with fire hoses, but downstairs as a matron escorted Little Lynn through the hallway, two of them—the sculptor of the pair brandishing his realistic creation—met them. "They're after me," Little Lynn gasped as she swooned into the matron's arms.

The escaping Clarence Gregory had taken Deputy Ruth Thornton hostage, jamming the soap pistol to her side and passing a long line of spectators waiting to get inside the courtroom. When they met Wes Wise in the hall, Ruth Thornton warned him about the gun as they moved past him on their way toward the Main Street entrance. Wes was in the middle of things again, and George Phenix was soon upstairs with a camera. Before long Deputy Thornton was rescued and safe, Gregory's freedom and his sculpture career were over, and Little Lynn was revived in time to testify about a phone call and her twenty-five-dollar telegram. After a phone company witness corroborated her call to Ruby and a couple of character witnesses appeared, Joe B. Brown gaveled a weekend recess. March 6 had been a hell of a day in that courthouse, and thank God it was Friday.

Sheriff Bill Decker, who had been in the vanguard quelling rioting prisoners upstairs, was disgusted at the sideshow that had taken over his bailiwick. Dallas was looking bad again, and the sheriff, knowing how the national press had skewered his friend Jesse Curry, was cussing and wet from fire hoses as George Phenix watched him change his socks.

THE FUGUE STATE

Ruby's roommate George Senator testified the following Monday about Ruby's agitated behavior on the morning he shot Oswald, supporting Belli's contention that the defendant had acted in some unconscious "fugue state." Bill Alexander cross-examined Senator with damning questions about Ruby's pugnacious reputation: "He picked on drunks and women, didn't he?" And with controlled sarcasm, the assistant prosecutor danced around the inference that Ruby and Senator were a homosexual couple—in that day and place, a powerful hint to discredit both witness and defendant.

For some reason, Belli discredited his own next witness—another stripper, Patricia Kohs—by revealing that she'd been brought from jail, where she was being held on a drug charge. Since she hadn't been convicted, prosecutors couldn't have mentioned her charge or incarceration in court. But Belli's doing so weakened her account of Ruby's throwing a man down a flight of stairs, then beating the victim's head against the sidewalk only to stop as though he'd awakened from a trance.

One newsman testified that his radio station had announced the Oswald transfer for ten o'clock, although police had given most of us to understand that time to be intentionally inexact, only the earliest hour when we should be ready. Another played his tape of the shooting and testified that it would have included anything Ruby said as he lunged and fired, although the reporter had been shouting at Oswald at the moment, perhaps drowning out Ruby's epithet to which nearby officers had testified. Still another, a Top 40 radio guy who gave his employment as furniture salesman, testified that Ruby could have shot Oswald at the midnight press showup if he'd had his gun. Ruby had claimed that he'd been carrying it that night, but he later repudiated that statement as a lie intended to undermine the case for premeditation. He had been arrested more than once for carrying a concealed weapon, so he might have hesitated to enter police headquarters with the pistol under his coat that Friday night.

The National Epilepsy League had shown enough interest in the psychomotor defense to give reporters pamphlets casting doubt that seizures caused violence. The prosecution's cadre of noted neurologists and psychiatrists had testified that electroencephalograms and other evidence didn't support Belli's experts' contention that Ruby suffered from any form of epilepsy. Instead, some prosecution experts explained small abnormalities in the defendant's brain-wave pattern as probable results of his sleep deprivation and habitual drug use. Preludin was a well-known appetite suppressant akin to amphetamines, and Ambar, the brand of Benzedrine he took, was a powerful "upper" as well. Both were known to cause emotional tension and sleeplessness. Truckers who took "bennies" called them "West Coast Turnaround Pills," which allowed them to drive to the West Coast, turn around, and haul back to Texas without nodding off.

Friday the 13th was the last day of testimony, and with fanfares and rolling drums Belli brought in Dr. Frederic Gibbs of Chicago, who had founded America's science of electroencephalography. Tall, handsome and graying like a statesman, Dr. Gibbs asserted that Ruby's EEG pattern did indeed indicate psychomotor variant epilepsy and that certain epileptic seizures can on occasion trigger violence. But Bill Alexander, with craft behind his politeness, brought out in cross-examination that the doctor had resigned from the American EEG Society as something of a heretic, was certified by neither the American Board of Neurology nor the American Board of Psychiatry, wasn't licensed to practice medicine in his own home state, and had no opinion about Jack Ruby's mental state when he shot Oswald. Later Alexander commented to reporters outside the courtroom, "If they're so eager to examine his brain, we'll send it to them from Huntsville after the execution."

After Belli's redirect of Dr. Gibbs, both sides rested. Judge Brown turned and said, "Sheriff, you will retire the jury so the court may prepare the charge."

"One minute," Belli interrupted while Gibbs remained on the stand, "the judge may have a question, or the jury."

Although Joe B. Brown had joined Belli and Tonahill in mirthful hallway press conferences between early proceedings, his cordiality had by now expired along with his sense of humor. "I have none, and I'm sure the jury has none," he snapped, "and if they had any, I wouldn't ask them."

Phil Burleson scooped up his trial notes and headed for his office to prepare 134 objections to the judge's coming charge to the jury. It was midmorning, and when Belli tried to delay reading of the jury charge, Judge Brown groused, "The case will go to the jury tonight, and I don't give a damn when you finish arguing it."

MIDNIGHT ARGUMENTS

At eight o'clock that evening Judge Joe B. Brown read the charge to the jury, and seven lawyers began final arguments: Belli, Tonahill, and Burleson for the defense, and Wade, Alexander, Bowie, and the previously inconspicuous Frank Watts for the prosecution. We were allowed neither cameras nor microphones in the courtroom during these summations, the judge having reversed an earlier decision to allow the mikes at this final phase of the trial. However, the judge would permit a live television camera at the verdict. Back in our newsroom, Eddie was arranging the mobile trucks and cameras for a verdict that was to come sooner than observers had predicted.

Bill Alexander, who despite his fiendish look and sadistic humor, was a tough and skilled prosecutor, said that Ruby "has mocked American justice while the spotlight of the world is upon us. . . . American justice had Oswald in its possession. Oswald was entitled to the protection of the law . . . a living, breathing, American citizen . . . entitled to be tried in a court of justice." And Ruby sank into his chair as Alexander spun and pointed, "Just like you, Jack Ruby, who was his judge, his jury and his executioner! You denied him the very thing that you demand through your lawyer the loudest!"

The calm and polite Phil Burleson made the defense's only plea for a verdict of murder without malice, which would have drawn the light sentence that Tom Howard had wanted. "The only malice in this case," he said, "comes from the blistering lips of some police officers who didn't even make reports of what they saw and heard." Burleson was a scholarly lawyer, and the prosecution's Jim Bowie, also a strong scholar, answered him with a rebuttal based on law and precedent.

The lumbering Joe Tonahill, continuing to compare Bill Alexander's eyes—rather astutely—with a tarantula's, rambled on with a mixture of bombast and sentimentality: "I've seen men killed in action, buried at sea. . . . I've stood in the cemeteries at Guadalcanal, Guam, Okinawa, Luzon, where, as far as the eye could see, little white crosses—"

"Judge," Henry Wade finally interrupted, "I don't think there's anything in the record on Mr. Tonahill's war record, is there?"

The big East Texan droned on, "I've been furthermore privileged to work in this case with my friend Mel Belli. . . . I considered him my brother, a great man to sit at the elbow of, a wonderful humanitarian, a kind, thoughtful, considerate—"

It was getting late, and Wade had a bellyful of such stuff. "Judge, I don't think that's in the record either, what a great man Mr. Belli is. We object to it."

Friday the 13th had slipped away into Saturday morning when Belli began his baritone oratory, addressing "my brother Tonahill," the court, the state and the jury. "But let us see," he went on, "now in the beginning small hours of the morning, when great discoveries in the history of the world have been made in garrets and attics and basements, if here, in a temple of justice, we can't rediscover something that was never lost in your great city of Dallas—that we may rediscover justice."

Then Belli descended from unctuous eloquence to mention that he had dedicated his life to the law, "except for the months that Howard Naffziger wanted me to leave the law and go into his specialty of brain surgery."

Belli never mentioned to the jury that they had the option of finding his client guilty of the lesser charge of murder without malice, insisting instead on an either-or decision between acquittal and death. He tossed psychological terms at the jury, calling police testimony "confabulation"—replacement of memory gaps with falsifications they might have believed themselves—and describing his client's "fugue state," a lapse of consciousness that had surrounded Ruby's impulsive act.

Ruby sat impassive in the courtroom as Belli soiled the heroic image he'd imagined for himself: "Ah, great sport to have a character in the community. In the old days we used to call them, what? The village clown, the village idiot?" Belli began to speak more about himself and less about his client, name-dropping and courting those who would write his story. "Ah, ladies and gentlemen, I suppose that, before that handful of dust settles down on the plain to be scratched up by the dancing tumbleweed, that we'd all like to engrave our initials in some oak tree—that we'd like to be maybe in Bob Consodine's or Inez Robb's or Dorothy Kilgallen's column." Those three were sitting in their assigned courtroom seats, and Belli had brought in his own television producer, Sam Gallu, to document his performance.

Melvin Belli's oratory had brought the mammoth Tonahill to streaming tears, and the three-hundred-pound Jasper lawyer wiped his eyes like a weeping elephant as his friend thanked the jury repeatedly in closing. "You're an intelligent jury, and I don't butter you up," Belli said, spreading the margarine.

One o'clock loomed as Henry Wade stood to deliver the trial's last summation. The DA was coming down with the flu, and he knew that the jurors were tired too. Shortening his prepared argument, he pointed out the conflict in Belli's emphasizing his willingness to submit Ruby to EEGs while refusing to allow prosecutors' psychiatrists and neurologists to examine him, and he ridiculed Belli's reliance upon psychiatric jargon, particularly the notion of "'conflabberation,' or whatever that word is." Wade asked, "Do you want history to say that you fell for Mr. Belli's testimony here about the electroencephalograph?"

Wade had convinced twenty-four out of twenty-five capital juries to vote the death penalty, and he asked these twelve people to give Ruby the electric chair as a deterrent to those who might take the law into their own hands. "You can write a verdict in this case that will ring out all over this country and this nation and say you don't believe in this sort of thing . . . that we believe in the rule of law here—that we believe that democracy and the Bill of Rights, the things that we have all been raised on, still exist."

Henry Wade, after sixteen minutes of what he later called his career's worst closing argument, sat down at 1:07 A.M. Joe B. Brown glanced at the clock and instructed jurors that they would reconvene to choose a foreman and start deliberating at a decent hour. Then the judge said, "OK, Sheriff," and deputies returned Ruby to his cell upstairs. None of us had been allowed to interview him, but Wes had slipped him written questions through Joe Tonahill. Ruby had written in reply that he was "confused."

The defendant was not alone in his confusion, and he had heard Belli say "village idiot" more than once.

TV IN COURT

While the jury deliberated that morning, the street outside was awash in green, as the St. Patrick's Day Parade passed, held early on Saturday the 14th. Sardonic to the bone, assistant prosecutor Bill Alexander observed that Dallas was pushing its luck, considering the outcome of the city's last parade for an Irishman.

Knowing that juries are unpredictable, reporters were staying close to the courtroom. Our live bus, The Blue Goose, was outside at the curb, and our production crew had set up cameras in the courtroom and outside on the street. For the first time during the trial, we were to be allowed in the courtroom with both video and audio equipment. And perhaps for history's first time, a murder verdict would be televised live. "It's for posterity," the judge had said. Our crews were still setting up when word came that the jury was ready to deliver its verdict, two hours and nineteen minutes after it had reassembled that morning just after nine o'clock.

The no-longer-jolly Judge Brown adjusted his robe as he swept into the courtroom and took his seat. Nelson Benton held the live CBS mike, and I was taking notes as I squatted up front. Wes and other KRLD reporters were there on the job, along with our artists Ken Hansen, Gary Artzt and Chuck Fisher, whose drawings had given our viewers their look inside courtroom proceedings until this last day. The jury filed in, and foreman Max Causey handed Brown the verdict.

EPILEPSY ACQUITTED

If I had covered every session of the trial, I might have expected what was written on that slip of paper. But like many observers I flinched to hear the judge read without a trace of emotion, "We the jury find the defendant guilty of murder with malice as charged in the indictment and assess his punishment at death."

Immediately after Brown had droned out the jury's verdict, Melvin Belli burst out in the courtroom and unleashed a tirade against the verdict, the jury, and the entire population of Dallas. "This jury wasn't concerned even with listening to us in arguments. They had their minds made up!" In that accusation, Belli might have been right. His defense, based entirely upon the notion that Ruby suffered from the ill-defined psychomotor epilepsy, had sounded to the jury like mumbo-jumbo.

When a reporter asked him to repeat his statement, Belli shouted, "Repeat this? I'll repeat this with every breath I have in me for as long as I live! And I'll stop practicing law if we don't reverse this and make these people of Dallas ashamed of themselves!"

Media the world over had zeroed in on Dallas, and Belli was happy to blame the whole metropolis for the failure of his far-fetched defense scheme. "I hope the people of Dallas are proud of this jury that was shoved down our throats."

Belli accused the jury of disregarding all his expert psychological testimony, when the truth was that they simply had not believed it. Long after Judge Brown had dismissed the jury and ended the proceedings, Belli stood in the courtroom and continued his rant. As film cameras whirred, the King of Torts chipped away at the city's reputation: "And the blight that's on Dallas—that those few twelve people who announced the death penalty in this case—they'll make this a city of shame for evermore! And I'm going to participate in this skew when I write this appeal!"

CAMERAMEN ON THE FURNITURE

Scrambling for camera angles and recordings of the bedlam that had broken out, some reporters had jumped onto tables and chairs, and the jostling reminded me of the mess in police headquarters four months before. Joe B. Brown had left the room after adjourning the court, but he reappeared, outraged, and demanded a restoration of some decorum. Brown walked to the rear of the courtroom and ordered the live pool

Melvin Belli rants against Dallas after Ruby's guilty verdict as Joe Tonahill looks outraged and KRLD's Wes Wise, a future Dallas mayor, holds the mike. *Photograph courtesy AP/Wide World Photos*

operator to turn the camera off. Although Brown had wanted a live camera present at the verdict, there had been some misunderstanding about what kind of camera or cameras were to be allowed in the courtroom that day, and exactly when they could be there. As a result, the approval of one live pool camera was taken by some reporters to imply permission for movie and still cameras, and after the court was adjourned, the courtroom was suddenly full of them, along with audio recorders.

"I think the networks fell down on me this morning," Brown told CBS's Nelson Benton after the trial. "There was an agreement there would be no cameras in that courtroom except the one television camera. After I went in and took the verdict and walked out and came back in, there were all networks in there. Everybody was in there with a camera. . . . I made an agreement with you all; you should have kept it."

Judge Brown betrayed some uncertainty about the distinction between live television, 16 mm movie film cameras, and the strobe-lighted still cameras of the print media. He had left the courtroom immediately after adjourning the trial, only to receive a phone call in his office from a friend who had told him that the Belli diatribe was still in progress on the live camera. "You remember the agreement was we would cut the television off as soon as I left the bench," he went on as his geniality re-asserted itself. "Over all, Nelson, I don't mean to complain. I'm not a griper, I've been in public office too long. And I guess perhaps I shouldn't criticize you all for what you did, because over all you did a wonderful job, and I appreciate it a very great deal. Perhaps your zeal got away this morning. I don't know, I wasn't here. They woke me up . . . when the jury was ready, and I got up and showered and came on down here, and everything went off fine."

As the cameras and mikes left him in the courtroom, Belli moved his orations into the hallway, where Wes held our live mike as Belli went on, with Tonahill looking properly outraged beside him. Down the hall, Henry Wade gave the press a calm assessment of the case. "Well," he said, "I wasn't satisfied with my argument to the jury *a-tall* and felt aw-ful low about it last night." But with such a sudden verdict, he said, "I thought we had either life or death. I didn't know which."

Belli had used psychobabble words such as the "fugue state" suppos-edly triggered by his client's psychomotor epilepsy, and Wade couldn't resist the irony when asked about his adversary's shouting that the ver-dict was "the biggest disgrace in the history of American law." The hint of a smile crossed Wade's face as he said, "I think that's his 'fugue state' he's talking about. The way I saw him yelling and screaming up there, I believe it's the first time he ever lost a case."

Henry Wade had won twenty-five death penalties, and he summed this one up in his matter-of-fact terms. Noting that Belli had insisted upon the unconvincing insanity defense instead of pleading for leniency, he said, "I don't think Dallas was on trial, I don't think I was on trial, I don't think Belli was on trial, I think Jack Ruby was on trial. I think it was a murder case that had more implications probably than the ordinary killing, because of the fact you're killing a man, handcuffed, that's inno-cent until he's proven guilty."

Wade called Ruby's act an assassination and explained that the testi-mony of Pat Dean and other policemen had been the key to proving pre-meditation in the case. Ruby had told Pat that he'd thought of killing Oswald two days before he did so. He had boasted to several officers that he had intended to shoot him three times before L. C. Graves stopped the revolver's cylinder—and that he hoped he'd killed the son of a bitch.

To counter Belli's expert witnesses, Wade had brought in a handful of noted neurologists and psychiatrists who had read Ruby's electroencephalograms and doubted that psychomotor epilepsy had triggered that pistol. The D.A. countered Belli's accusation that the jury had disregarded his experts' testimony. "I think the jury listened to all of it. I've tried a number of cases where they had psychiatry as a defense, and I will say that I thought they put up as weak a psychiatric defense as I've ever seen."

Texas law required the defense to appeal any death verdict, but Melvin Belli wouldn't be the one to do it. He would eventually file an *amicus* brief in the appeal, but after his post-verdict tirade in the courtroom, the Ruby family fired him. Later they stopped him from selling *Life* magazine the snapshots of Ruby he'd smuggled out of the jail on the day after the verdict.

In the extended days of Ruby's motions, hearings, the trial itself, then post-verdict shuffling of defense lawyers and more ensuing motions and hearings, Phil Burleson became a friend to me and some of the other reporters. While the Belli–Tonahill show was on stage, Phil was the defense team member who'd taken time to explain to us just what all the shouting in court was about. Unlike the flamboyant Belli and Tonahill, Burleson had reminded the jury that they could find Ruby guilty of murder without malice, as Tom Howard, a low-profile attorney without a law library, had hoped that a jury might.

9
The Last of "Sparky" Ruby

BOB HUFFAKER

Jack Ruby was under sentence of death, and the would-be patriot had heard his defense counsel compare him to a "village idiot." Now the remnants of his strange little existence were ebbing away in jail as he waited out appeals, motions, and hearings. His family, having sent Belli back to San Francisco in a hurry, began looking for a heavyweight to lead the defense through the appellate phase. Getting rid of Tonahill took them longer, since he insisted upon staying on the case with Phil Burleson. At one proceeding to fire the colorful giant, Ruby was cursing him before reporters while, down the hall, Tonahill was waxing eloquent about his own loyalty and determination to protect "that boy."

Jack Ruby's brother Earl consulted Sol Dann, a fellow Detroit resident who practiced civil law, and Dann agreed to help the family find a new chief defense counsel. For a fleeting sixteen hours, they had Percy Foreman, Texas's best-known criminal defense lawyer, on the job. But Dann and Ruby's family, shocked at the mess that Belli had made of the case, insisted upon micromanaging the Houston attorney's handling of matters, and Foreman resigned, with a parting shot at Sol Dann's interference and a note of sympathy to Ruby.

Foreman's departure previewed several similar short-lived representations by a handful of excellent attorneys who wouldn't countenance the family's meddling in the case. Dr. Hubert Winston Smith left as pro bono counsel because the University of Texas Law School had threatened to stop his faculty pay, and he was followed by Dallas attorneys Clayton Fowler and Emmett Colvin, then Charles A. Bellows of Chicago. At one point, Sol Dann had fired Fowler, who had responded by firing Dann.

Mutual firings among the defense team complicated matters, and their protracted attempt to remove Tonahill tangled the situation further.

Six days after the death verdict, Burleson and Tonahill had filed a motion with Brown's court for a new trial, asking the judge to reverse himself on four points: denial of venue change, refusal to disqualify jurors who'd seen the crime on television, denial of a last-ditch defense request for a sanity hearing, and allowing police testimony about Ruby's post-arrest statements.

Sol Dann soon brought two nationally known lawyers to the case. The first was William Kuntzler of New York, the famous civil rights advocate who had represented Martin Luther King and the Rosenbergs and had published landmark books in his field. The second was Elmer Gertz, a noted Chicago generalist who was about to publish a book about his gaining parole for Nathan Leopold. On March 19, Dann, Gertz, Kuntzler, and Sam Houston Clinton of the Texas Civil Liberties Union went to federal court with Phil Burleson and Joe Tonahill in a failed attempt to disqualify Judge Joe B. Brown—and, in a tense atmosphere, to eliminate the discredited yet tenacious Joe Tonahill from the defense team. The federal court prohibited cameras and restricted reporters' movements, unlike the free access we had enjoyed during state proceedings.

The fight between Sol Dann and Joe Tonahill marked some of the dirtiest moments in the legal wrangling that surrounded this case. Tonahill had attacked Kuntzler for representing "the Communist element in this country." He even referred in writing to "Sol Dann and his fellow ghouls," and after one particularly ugly shouting match, Dann accused the East Texan of anti-Semitism.

The federal court tossed the matter of Ruby's legal counsel back to the Texas Court of Criminal Appeals, the equivalent of the state's supreme court in criminal matters. That appellate court deferred judgments until the trial court had settled the issue of just who the hell was representing Jack Ruby, who had told the federal court, "I never had any defense in court." Phil Burleson, the straight shooter, was the only defense counsel who stuck to the case all along without anyone's objection.

Judge Brown's loose judicial conduct led Phil Burleson to move that he disqualify himself from further proceedings in the case. Brown had presided over a courtroom circus, posing for photographers and getting caught reading a comic book on the bench. But the final straw that brought Burleson's motion was the discovery that Brown was producing a book about the case which might actually have been released while appellate motions were still before him. At first Brown resisted, but when a letter from him to his publisher surfaced, he at last withdrew from the case in June 1965.

After Judge Brown was replaced by Judge Louis Holland of Montague County, the court's act was cleaned up, and proceedings became orderly. But time was slipping away from Jack Ruby, and attorneys from both prosecution and defense had agreed that he needed psychiatric care.

THE EMOTIONAL DECLINE OF JACK RUBY

Six weeks after he was sentenced to the electric chair, Ruby was showing signs of wild delusions, paranoia and suicidal impulses. Sheriff Decker had treated his star prisoner with kindness, inviting a few of Ruby's old friends to visit him in jail and assigning a constant guard to prevent the convicted killer from harming himself. But on Sunday morning, April 26, Decker told me of an incident that had taken place in the early morning hours, and I reported it on CBS radio: "Dallas County Sheriff Bill Decker has confirmed that Jack Ruby made an unsuccessful suicide attempt this morning. The sheriff said Ruby had refused to go to bed; he'd been sitting in his cell talking with the guard who watches him twenty-four hours a day. Ruby asked the guard for a drink of water, and when the officer stepped out of the cell, the condemned slayer of Lee Oswald got up and rammed his head against the cell wall." The jailer had hurried in to stop him, the jail doctor had examined him immediately, and deputies had taken him for X-rays. Sheriff Decker said that Ruby had suffered only a knot on his head and never lost consciousness. But after apparently attempting suicide, he had tried to tear his clothing into strips to make a noose. As CBS radio was airing my report, Dr. Louis J. West, a University of Oklahoma psychiatry professor, was conferring with Ruby in an interview room, and Decker ordered Ruby's cell cleared out for his safety. "The bed has been removed from the cell now," I reported, "and he has only a mattress. Ruby will be in the legal limelight again tomorrow morning when his attorneys seek his transfer to a hospital for more mental tests."

Ruby, meanwhile, was telling Dr. West that the nation's Jews were being slaughtered in retaliation for his crime and that his brother Sam had been tortured, mutilated and burned in the street outside the jail. Dr. West diagnosed him as having fallen into suicidal paranoia. While spouting wild delusions, Ruby had insisted that he wasn't insane—reinforcing, in Catch-22 logic, the psychiatrist's opinion that he was, by now.

The next day Judge Brown denied the motion to hospitalize Ruby but said that he would order a sanity hearing. No one was mentioning anything about psychomotor epilepsy.

THE WARREN COMMISSION COMES TO DALLAS

One week after the assassination, President Lyndon Johnson, by executive order, had created the President's Commission on the Assassination of President John F. Kennedy, which, with Supreme Court Chief Justice Earl Warren as its chairman, became known as the Warren Commission. Its seven distinguished members, from both political parties, met six days later and got down to business. The FBI and Secret Service were already furnishing them initial investigative reports before Christmas, and the commission had been assembling testimony, depositions, affidavits and other evidence. But they had waited for Ruby's verdict before questioning those of us whose testimony might either interfere with his right to a fair trial or compromise investigative and legal proceedings in Oswald's murder.

The FBI and Secret Service had interviewed me and other witnesses in the Oswald shooting soon after the crime, and their reports gave the Warren Commission its starting point for questioning us. After Ruby's trial, we began receiving our subpoenas. Ten days after the verdict, Sergeant Patrick Trevore Dean walked up the steps of the Post Office Building to give Warren Commission counsels his sworn deposition. Pat's testimony about Ruby's statements in the jail had been strong evidence for the verdict of murder with malice, but he had no idea what a strange confrontation awaited him.

ACCUSATIONS OF PERJURY

Burt Griffin, one of the Warren Commission's two assistant counsels assigned to investigate Ruby's shooting of Oswald, had suspected that police were lying about Ruby's statements after his arrest. These were the officers whose testimony had convicted Melvin Belli's client of murder with malice, and something had convinced Griffin that Pat Dean was lying about what Ruby had told him in jail after Pat's interview with Tom Pettit and me down in the garage.

Griffin, a young former U.S. attorney from Ohio, had read Pat's interviews with FBI agents. He also knew that Pat had testified to what Ruby had told him in jail after he'd shot Oswald: that he'd come down the Main Street ramp—and that he'd decided to kill Oswald when he saw him in the assembly room two nights earlier. But Griffin thought that Pat was lying about both statements.

At that time, Griffin was apparently placing too much stock in a story that Ruby had come in from the jail office while helping push a television camera into the garage. Investigations would disprove that rumor, one of several spawned amid the confusion after the shooting as officers tried to guess where he'd come from. More doubt arose when a reservist claimed to have seen Ruby wearing a maroon jacket at the railing before he lunged out to shoot Oswald. That reserve officer, perhaps a tad too eager to remember, listed his regular job as real estate salesman.

In Central Texas a few years before, I'd worked as a reservist to learn more about police reporting, and I'd found myself among guys who liked to dress up and play cops and robbers. The Dallas reservists were no more professional than I'd been, and their eagerness to be part of the story might have overstimulated their memories. Trying to explain the reservist's unsupported account of the maroon jacket, officers had concluded that I was the fellow he'd seen. I have never worn a maroon jacket.

Another reservist told a similarly belated and vague tale of seeing Ruby descend the ramp, and Burt Griffin called him "a damned liar" to his face. Griffin had come to suspect the worst of the Dallas police, and reservists' cowboy testimony stoked his doubts about Pat's honesty.

Secret Service chief Forrest Sorrels's inability to confirm Ruby's statements didn't clarify matters either. The sixty-three-year-old Sorrels had delayed more than two months before writing his report on the matter, and his later testimony before Warren Commission hearings in Washington revealed memory gaps that left Pat's testimony in limbo. Sorrels had even forgotten that the officer who sent Pat to escort him to the jail was Chief Curry himself.

More doubt about Ruby's having come down the ramp had risen during the confusion after the shooting when Tom Pettit had thrust his NBC

mike between two veteran Juvenile Bureau officers and Assistant Chief
Charles Batchelor as they were trying to figure how the gunman had gotten at Oswald. Detective Roy Lowery, who had been at the wall near the
jail office, told Batchelor, "This man came from behind this camera—or
this corner—out of the crowd and just dove out of the crowd."

Officer William "Blackie" Harrison then told Batchelor about what he
had not really seen, saying, "He came from behind that car, that green
car there. He jumped over the railing. I saw the gun." He had seen the
gun, but only at the last split second.

Having heard his guess, Tom Pettit went on to state several times
that the assailant had come out of the green sedan parked near our live
camera. But both Harrison and Lowery testified to Warren Commission counsels Leon Hubert and Burt Griffin that they had not seen
Ruby at all before he lunged out to fire. Lowery, who never claimed to
have seen how Ruby actually got into the crowd, only that he'd come
"from behind this camera or this corner," had been part of the initial
speculation that Ruby had entered pushing a TV camera. The Warren
Commission eventually accepted the truth of Ruby's statements about
his means of entry.

But early in taking depositions, Griffin distrusted the police, and he
doubted that Ruby had admitted deciding to kill Oswald when he saw
the assassin at the midnight showup. Ruby had bragged that he'd known
he was going for Oswald when he'd seen "that smirk on his face" before
the cameras, and Pat might have misunderstood which Oswald photo
opportunity he'd meant. Belli had argued that Ruby, having been armed
at the midnight showup, could have shot Oswald then, but Ruby would
later confess to Earl Warren that he'd lied about carrying his pistol that
night. The Sunday transfer, then, would have been his first chance to
get a shot at Oswald. Such issues were unresolved when Sergeant Dean
appeared before Griffin, who hadn't yet questioned Blackie Harrison
and Roy Lowery.

At eight o'clock on Tuesday evening, March 24, when Pat entered
Room 301 of the Post Office Building, Burt Griffin was waiting for him.
Griffin began in a personable tone, and Patrick Dean responded in kind.
Some of the deposition questions concerned what Pat had told Tom Pet-
tit and me after the shooting. Mistaken reports had said that he'd identi-
fied Jack Ruby by name in our live interview, but in those moments after

Ruby had been subdued and arrested, I hadn't asked the assailant's name before Pat could release it. Another false rumor about that hasty interview was that Dean had claimed to have seen Ruby come down the Main Street ramp. Pat was concerned about being misquoted, and he tried to clarify the matters with Griffin.

Griffin continued polite questioning for a couple of hours, then sent the court reporter out and talked to the sergeant off the record. Since Pat had testified to Ruby's statements in the murder trial, and since he was under oath in his deposition to Griffin, accusing him of lying was also accusing him of perjury. And despite his friendly tone, that is what Burt Griffin did.

A few days later, Griffin wrote to his superiors, "I tried to approach him on a basis of respect and friendship while maintaining a certain distance. I said, however, that I did not believe his testimony in some respects but that I thought I understood why it was that he was not making the truthful statement which I believed possible."

Later, having demanded a Washington hearing, Pat told the Warren Commission, "Well, after the court reporter left, Mr. Griffin started talking to me in a manner of gaining my confidence, in that he would help me and that he felt I would probably need some help in the future. . . . My not knowing what he was building up to, I asked Mr. Griffin to go ahead and ask me what he was going to ask me. He continued to advise me that he wanted me to listen to what he had to say before he asked me whatever question he was going to ask me. I finally told him that whatever he wanted to ask me he could just ask me, and if I knew I would tell him the truth or if I didn't know, I would tell him I didn't know."

Young Burt Griffin was trying to sort out inconsistencies that included Pat's underestimate of the time between Ruby's shot and his statements in the jail. But Griffin was on shaky ground to accuse such a trusted officer of lying—and lying under oath, at that. Pat Dean could hardly believe what was happening at first, as Griffin himself wrote to the commission counsel: "He said he didn't understand what I had in mind since he had tried to be extremely truthful and I believe he then asked me to explain what I had in mind."

Pat told the commission what happened next. "And then very dogmatically he said that, 'Jack Ruby didn't tell you that he entered the basement via the Main Street ramp.' And of course I was shocked at this. This is what I testified to, in fact. I was cross-examined on this, and he, Mr. Griffin, further said, 'Jack Ruby did not tell you that he had thought or planned to kill Oswald two nights prior.' And then he said, 'Your testimony was false, and these reports to your chief of police are false.'"

Pat told the commission that Griffin had refused to explain why he doubted him but had said that cross-examination could prove his accusations. "That is when I told Mr. Griffin that these are the facts and I can't change them. . . . I quoted Ruby just about verbatim, and since he didn't believe me, and I was saying they were true, we might as well terminate the interview."

Pat had come to the deposition with unrelated information which eventually proved of no consequence, and he insisted in presenting it to Griffin despite his anger. Pat was outraged that his twelve-year police career was under attack, and he walked out into the night determined to fight back. Pat had organized basement security, then had hurdled a police car trying to protect the prisoner, all in vain, and he wasn't going to suffer this insult.

Neither was Henry Wade. By accusing the DA's star witness of lying, Griffin was attacking the basis for the prosecutor's case for murder with malice, only ten days after the verdict. Pat Dean offered to take a polygraph examination. Then through his supervisors, he took his complaint to the district attorney. Wade went straight to U.S. District Judge Barefoot Sanders, and within four days J. Lee Rankin, the Warren Commission's general counsel, had ordered Burt Griffin out of Dallas.

The next morning after Griffin had overplayed his hand with Pat Dean, Detective Roy Lowery testified to counsel Leon Hubert, "The first time I saw Ruby he was lunging, and almost instantaneously the shot was fired, and I couldn't say that I saw him come from the crowd. I saw a blur, and about this time the shot was fired, and there is Jack Ruby right in front of me." Lowery, who had been only four feet from the attack, had held down one of Ruby's legs while officers shook him down on the jail office floor.

Later on the day of Lowery's deposition, Burt Griffin had grilled Blackie Harrison at great length under oath, trying to confirm his suspicion that Pat Dean had perjured himself. "Did you at any time, now, did you see Jack Ruby in this basement at any time before he shot Oswald?"

"Not before he shot Oswald."

"When you were standing here [indicating a basement diagram], did you feel a man pressing up against your back?"

"No, I didn't."

By then Harrison had known for months that photos showed Ruby standing at his back before plunging between him and George Phenix. A stocky man, Blackie had moved fast. "Well, I grabbed him and more or less went to the floor with him, and then we took him on into the jail office."

"And how long did you remain with him in the jail office?"

"Until he was handcuffed, and I went upstairs on the elevator with him."

Blackie had left Ruby with officers Don Archer, Tom McMillon, and Barnard Clardy to return to the basement, where he and Roy Lowery tried to explain the attack to Assistant Chief Charles Batchelor in the presence of Tom Pettit's mike.

On March 25, Burt Griffin was pressing him hard: "Did you talk to anybody while you were up there, or before you got up there, concerning how Ruby got into the basement?"

"No; I told Chief Batchelor, just after I came back downstairs from taking him up—I told Chief Batchelor that I thought he came from behind those cameras over there, but—and that is where I thought he came from at that time."

"Now, why did you think he came from behind the cameras?"

"Well, there was—he came from my left, and I don't see how he could get down the ramp."

"Why did you feel that way?"

"Well, I knew there was an officer on the ramp, and I just didn't feel like he could have gotten down there."

"Did you also feel that you would have seen him if he had come down that ramp?"

"No, not necessarily; because I wasn't looking toward the ramp all of the time."

Burt Griffin, a bright and gutsy inquisitor, might have placed more credence in Pat Dean's word if he'd talked to Harrison and Lowery first. But his zeal had earned him a ticket out of Texas.

On April Fools' Day, Griffin's surviving co-counsel, Leon Hubert, finished taking Pat Dean's deposition. "There was just no putting them in the same room, that's all there was to it," Hubert put it delicately.

REPORTING UNDER OATH

When Leon Hubert took my deposition two weeks later, Burt Griffin had been safely in Washington since Easter, far away from one cop who could jump over cars and would've liked to whip his ass. My floor director, Bob Hankal, had just finished his deposition when I showed up at Post Office Room 301. It was half past four in the afternoon, and George Phenix was going to be next, in the same room where Dean and Griffin had clashed.

Leon Hubert, a slight, balding and gentlemanly attorney, got right down to business and impressed me by his polite and direct manner. With a nod he had me take a seat at a heavy oak table, near a big scale model of the police garage. He informed me of the commission's legal authority, took my oath, then ran me through the FBI reports filed by agents Hardin and Rawlings and by Pinkston and Brown. After I had corrected minor glitches in both reports, Hubert had me point to places on the mockup of the basement garage: where I was standing, where Jim English's camera was set up, where others stood, and so forth. On a map that corresponded to the model, he had me mark the various locations and initial them, and he asked me details of what I had seen and heard.

Other than confirming the mechanics of the murder and the ensuing pandemonium, my testimony was insignificant, but I tried to get it right.

"When did you first observe that something had happened?"

"When I heard the shot, I recognized it as the sound of a .38, and as soon as reflexes would do it, I turned and saw Oswald as he fell. I really could not distinguish Ruby from the mass of humanity that was there, but the thing that I saw when I turned around was Oswald falling."

Leon Hubert and I stood, and with his guidance I estimated that Oswald had been eleven feet from me at the moment of the shot. "Did you hear anything at any time after?"

"Yes, sir, I did. . . . I heard Police Officer Richard Swain, who was— I don't know where he was before the shot was fired, but immediately afterward, he was standing a very short distance from me blocking access of anyone else, and he made—he shouted for no one to come any further."

"You don't remember the words?"

"The words. Frankly, I think he said, 'I'll knock you on your ass,' but I'm not certain exactly what the words were."

"But in any case, in the sense you understood the officer, he was trying to keep anybody from converging there?"

"And how. Yes, he was."

I left the deposition room thinking that the investigation was in good hands, with meticulous probing and even a dandy plywood scale model. I had no idea of the myriad problems that dogged the Warren Commission, not the least of which was wobbly communication between its Ruby detail—Griffin and Hubert—and its general counsel, J. Lee Rankin.

The commission staff had to depend upon investigations by the slippery FBI. Although Chief Jesse Curry had told me on national television the day after the assassination that the FBI had known of Oswald's history and whereabouts, its Dallas chief, J. Gordon Shanklin, had ordered a coverup. Agent James Hosty said that Shanklin—another fed who parted his name on the side like J. Edgar Hoover—ordered him to destroy a threatening note Oswald had delivered personally to their office not many days before he shot the president. J. Edgar himself used tactics that prevented Griffin and Hubert from being told that Ruby had been an FBI informant—albeit one of little significance. Nor were they given other information known to some commission members that might have helped their efforts to draw the big picture. Both assistant commission counsels were excluded when Earl Warren himself came to Dallas.

WARREN, RUBY, AND OSWALD'S RIFLE

Security was tight on Sunday morning, the 7th of June, 1964, when Earl Warren's plane landed at Love Field. A transport aircraft also taxied in from the runway, and a Cadillac limousine rolled down a ramp dropped from beneath its tail. The big open car was built to specifications like those of the Lincoln that had carried JFK from that same tarmac to his death six months before.

This sudden arrival was a surprise, kept secret until the planes were on the ground, and calculated to draw minimal notice on a quiet spring Sabbath. Dallas was its usual sleepy Sunday self when Warren slipped into the city with an entourage and a limousine that would become a mock moving target that day.

U.S. Representative Gerald Ford, later to replace Richard Nixon as president, flew in with the chief justice, along with commission general counsel J. Lee Rankin and assistant counsel Arlen Specter, now a U.S. senator. There were plenty of Secret Service agents along, and with the help of Dallas police they blocked off Elm Street and staged a series of drive-by enactments of the assassination. Earl Warren and other commission members sighted into the scope of Lee Oswald's unloaded rifle, worked the bolt and squeezed off dry-firings while agents brought the limousine past at the speed of JFK's ill-fated car. Warren and others got a firsthand feel for the rifle and the target, training the scope's crosshairs on the agent sitting in the car's right rear seat—the place of honor reserved for the president.

After the reenactments, police reopened Elm Street to regular traffic, and the cadre of investigators went to a jury-deliberation room that Sheriff Decker had prepared for them on short notice. They were going to talk to Jack Ruby. Texas Attorney General Waggoner Carr had sent his two representatives in the investigation, Robert G. Storey and Leon Jaworski, later to be Richard Nixon's nemesis as Watergate special prosecutor.

One unfortunate weakness of the Warren Commission's investigation was that its working staff, including Burt Griffin and Leon Hubert, were not privy to Ruby's brief role as an FBI informant and to CIA efforts to assassinate Fidel Castro. Griffin and Hubert were conspicuously absent at the commission's meeting with Ruby, where Congressman Gerald Ford, with better intelligence information than theirs, tried with little success to get more information from Ruby about Cuba. Most of the interview was wasted on Ruby's ramblings and requests that he be transferred to Washington.

Ruby begged for a polygraph test, which he later got, and it was printed in the Warren Report but dismissed as unreliable. I talked to Joe Tonahill after the three-hour conference, then fed Robert Trout at the CBS radio news desk: "Tonahill," I reported, "said Ruby and Warren shook hands when they met and as they parted. Tonahill described Ruby's behavior as very humble but expressed doubt about the condemned man's ability to answer the questions."

Tonahill had told me that Ruby had been wide-eyed and staring, sometimes neither responsive nor coherent. Entering the deliberation room with the Supreme Court's chief justice, the huge East Texas lawyer had given his customary greeting to the room's air vents, with his usual implication that Decker had bugged the place.

A DISPUTED INTERVIEW:
RUBY'S CONSPIRACY THEORY

Jack Ruby's first wish when he testified to Earl Warren and the others on June 7 had been for a lie detector test, and when the Warren Report came out in late September 1964, Ruby was bitterly disappointed that psychiatrists had thrown doubt upon his polygraph results—and upon his sanity. He railed about coverups and conspiracies, and the next time I met him on the way to the courtroom in our familiar hallway dance, he was ready to denounce the Warren Report and to vent grievances and suspicions.

Encountering this pale and deteriorating little prisoner was like coming face-to-face with the Man in the Iron Mask—a man perpetually locked away out of sight, then suddenly dragged up from the dungeon into the light of day. Ruby seemed to feel the hopelessness of his situation as his days ticked away, and he was eager to be heard, especially after the Warren Report discounted his polygraph exam. His attorneys wanted him to shut up, but Jack wanted to talk, and we reporters were going to let him.

Ruby had spoken to another station that morning, and our sound cameraman Dan Garza had caught hell from Eddie Barker for missing Ruby's comments before the early session with Judge Brown. I was working the morning police beat and doing the noon radio news, so I had not been covering the hearings. At 12:15, I was off duty after my last newscast, but the Old Captain was furious at being scooped. So I headed over to the courthouse determined to get an interview with Ruby.

I got there just in time to catch a brief response from Ruby as he was taken to lunch; then Dan Garza and I had an hour to plan our tactics for his return. At that time, television reporters were still permitted in the courtroom before the judge had taken the bench, and I knew that the judge was usually late. We could enter the courtroom as long as the judge had not called the hearing to order, and I planned to keep the mike in front of Ruby as long as he wanted to talk.

I would start the interview in the hallway dance, then follow Ruby to his seat at the front of the courtroom. A sound cameraman from another station was there, and since local reporters cooperated with each other, we choreographed the dance to include him. "All right, you guys now, get yourselves organized," I told them, and the three of us planned how I would walk to Ruby's left while they crawfished ahead of us on his right. I can't recall who the other cameraman was, but I think that he had to tape his mike to his camera and point it alongside his lens, a common practice with sound cameramen who had no mike man. I can't claim any keen journalistic skill in this act: I was there to hold the mike—and to address Jack Ruby in a respectful tone instead of shouting questions at the doomed prisoner.

Dan talked things over with the other cameraman while I paced with the mike. In the last seconds before Ruby emerged, I reminded them of our choreography. "All right. Get ready," I told them, then spoke into the mike, "Here comes Ruby now. Jack, I'd like to talk to you just a little bit. I'm Bob Huffaker, with KRLD."

"Yeah, I'm pretty close to KRLD," he said, "I've always been."

"You know Wes pretty well."

"Yeah," he said as we continued our brisk walk toward the courtroom.

"I wanted to ask you about—what do you think about the authenticity of the Warren Report?"

"Very—" he began, then turned to one of his protesting attorneys, "Will you please leave me alone, please?" We walked in through the open courtroom doors and up to the defense table, where Ruby sat down along with his attorneys, near Sol Dann.

"Sam doesn't want you to," Dann pleaded with him, apparently referring to Ruby's brother. They were determined to stop his public statements, but he insisted upon speaking as they continued to protest.

"Let me tell you this, the Warren Re—" he began again, then turned and snapped at Dann, "Will you quit getting excited? I'm handling my own—I know what I'm doing."

"Go ahead, Jack," I said.

"And the result is—"

Dann moved in and addressed my microphone: "You have no right. Counsel objects."

"I beg your pardon," I said, as Dann and Elmer Gertz continued to interrupt. "Sir, may we have your permission?"

"No."

"I want to," Ruby told Dann, his tragic temper flashing, "I'm going to walk out of the goddamned court in a minute." Sol Dann seemed to relent, as Ruby continued, "The Warren Report never gave me the true authencity [*sic*] when I requested a polygraph test, there was a little small article in small type that stated due to the fact that Mr. Ruby's—" and here he was interrupted with another plea.

"Sam, I insist upon getting this over with. Will you let me please do this? Let me get this over with. I want to get this out. Please."

"You've already said these things a dozen times," Sol Dann said.

"They never released the results of my polygraph test that was deleted from the Warren Report. Why was that deleted, I don't know why. I insisted on the polygraph right from the beginning. As a matter of fact, certain questions I created and originated that they would ask me at the time. They spent nine hours with me at the time, and yet the finality, the finality of the results of the test, they stated they refused to divulge the answers that I had given whether they were true or false, due to the fact of my mental condition. Because of that they feel that we cannot divulge the results of it. Why they held back the answers and to give their results, as to whether they're true or false, that's for you to find out." Jack Ruby was tipping off the press, again.

In that discounted polygraph examination, Ruby had continued to insist that he had entered the basement by the Main Street ramp when Rio Pierce drove out. He seemed to be trying to set matters straight. But as I knelt before him in the courtroom, his attorneys were fidgeting as he spouted off for the cameras. "And of all the complete Warren Report, that would either vindicate me as to my—if there was any conspiracy or if I had any premeditated thought prior to that Sunday morning—that would either vindicate me or implicate me. And I know in my heart and my soul when I insisted upon that polygraph test, that's what I wanted to bring out to the world, and to the American people that were waiting for that to happen.

"And I know that, being incarcerated for the length of time I've been in, and people are trying to bring out a false image about me that I'm not of sound mind, that is a little bit towards, towards the—being a part of insane or whatever they may say about it, my mind is more adept, more mature, more alert than it's ever been during my whole lifetime of years. So why would they make a statement like that, I don't know. That's for you to find out. And the whole question behind all this is what are the true and false answers of the polygraph test that I spent nine hours with the FBI and the Internal Rev—whoever they represented—for all that length of time. Why did they start to give me the tests in the first place if they didn't think I was capable of answering the questions whether it would be true or false. That's a very important item for you folks to remember, and, after this is all over, that's the thought should be in your mind.

"One more thought I want to bring out. Me in the inside, you gentlemen feel that I have no cognizance [he accented the word's second syllable] of what's happening. I would like to state this is a very important thing to remain in history for years and many years to come. The deceased person that I had—fatally—had made it so. It's certainly strange for a man that had never worked in all his years, suddenly had the capability of securing a job—a week—weeks prior to our beloved president coming to Dallas. Where did he get the information to know what was going to occur, and why suddenly he was so eager to go to work at this particular place, the most ideal place where to commit the terrible crime he had committed? A very wonderful thought for you folks to remember, after this is all over."

Jack was getting wound up. "Where in the high-up sources of our political regime did this despicable person get that knowledge what was going to happen and where the route was going to be taking place? I repeat this again: he had worked in that place three weeks prior to anyone knowing that the president had anticipated making this trip. Where else could he get that information? Think that over, gentlemen."

The judge was due any minute when I asked, "Jack, is this interview granted with your full cooperation and knowledge?"

Dann and Gertz interjected, "Over the objection of counsel," and several other protests. Nothing like this confrontation could happen in a modern courtroom, and I knew that I was at the very edge of legal ethics. I ignored these skilled and principled attorneys as I tilted the mike toward Ruby again. "The reason why I say I grant this, someone is trying to make a false image of me. As I repeat, my mind is as sound as it ever has been. And I don't want to fool anybody, I never intended to. And no one, no one—someone is trying to, rather, make other people believe that due to the cause of my incapacity of thinking correctly, that what I have to state and what answers I give won't be the true answers. Well, that's where the terrible tragedy has come in. Because I know what I'm saying and I know what I'm talking about. I know there's a terrible conspiracy in this world at this moment, and unfortunately for me, I happen to be the scapegoat to walk into traps to make that possible. Now if I stated my words verbatim, that's the words I intend to use."

Sol Dann said, "I think as his lawyer I should request you not to use this or anything that he has said in view of his condition. And in view of the objections that Mr. Gertz and I made to your interrogating him under these circumstances."

I continued to ignore the attorneys and address their client. "Jack, may I ask you, is this granted with your full knowledge, cooperation and permission?"

The lawyers were shouting objections to me, as he answered, "Yes."

"You have no moral or legal right, and you'll take the consequences," Dann told me, as Ruby interrupted.

"In the first place, you gentlemen have a right to judge as to whether I'm incoherent and I haven't my full faculties. I feel—I don't want to be—I don't want to be warped," he went on over a chorus of lawyers' arguments, "or harnessed, that I can't speak my true feelings, my true sensitivities as I want to. And perhaps someone may have a legal technicality in wanting to prevent me from saying it, I don't know what the hell motive is. But I'm speaking the truth," he said, his old Chicago street dialect surfacing as he pronounced it "troot," "with reference to the Warren Report, with reference to the last little episode I spoke about—about this person that happened to be fortunate enough to get a job weeks before our beloved president had even in his own mind anticipated coming to Dallas. Where did this person get this information to seek a job in that particular place?

"The reason why I'm saying all these things with reference to—evidently, everyone's taking it for granted that I'm cleared by the Warren Report. That I'm cleared—You already tried to object and—" he said as Sol Dann finally got the floor.

"I know it," Dann said to him. "These people don't have the moral or legal right of—"

"The world has a right to hear the truth!" Ruby shot back.

"You have attorneys. And while you have attorneys, you should listen occasionally to them."

"All right, you've said your piece," Ruby told Dann, who turned and spoke to me.

"I don't think you ought to be able to—I think you are acting in—with complete impropriety. A man is entitled to a fair hearing. A fair hearing does not include the intervention of the press over the objection of counsel. We have good moral and legal reasons why we think this should be confined to the courtroom. That's been one of the difficulties in this case. Too much has been out of the courtroom. This is something that should be decided according to American system of justice and fair play and due process. It should not be tried by newspaper and other publicity people who are not interested, necessarily, in arriving at—"

I interrupted him. "Sir, with your permission. There was one interview granted this morning, to another station."

"Well, there—no, no interviews were granted," he said as Dan Garza and I moved my mike cord and made way for our quick departure. Jack nodded and said good-bye as we left and Judge Brown took the bench.

This strange scene would not happen in these days—at least not anywhere above the dregs of cheap courtroom "reality" television. Sol Dann was right in trying to staunch his client's public ramblings. But I was abiding by Brown's court rules, even if I was foiling some dedicated attorneys.

With Ruby's permissions on record, I evaded a lawsuit, and the interview won KRLD News that year's Texas Association of Broadcasters' award, among others. Legal questions aside, Dan Garza and I were giving Jack Ruby a chance to be heard, for better or worse. More than anything else, Jack wanted to be understood as a sane patriot instead of a mentally disturbed killer. He had his own vague conspiracy theories, and he wanted his voice to project beyond the Dallas County Jail, which would turn out to be the last home he would have.

JACK WINS

At 10:30 on the morning of October 5, 1966, Jack Ruby's faithful attorney Phil Burleson entered Section 6M of Dallas County Jail, a spacious but lonely domain where Jack was the only prisoner. "Jack, you won!" he yelled.

Jack Ruby, sitting in white prison coveralls, looked up from the book he was reading and took the news with serenity. The Texas Court of Criminal Appeals had just granted him a new trial, reversing Judge Brown on two points: failure to transfer the sensational trial out of Dallas and failure to bar testimony of Pat Dean and other officers about statements Ruby made in custody. Phil explained to Jack that the ruling—a predictable one—meant that he might even get out of that damned cell on bond and remain free while lawyers prepared to defend him again.

I was on the radio desk, delivering five-minute newscasts on the hour and assembling stories for the fifteen-minute noon news. KRLD's clear-channel 1080 AM signal blanketed Texas and reached beyond the Rockies. From Austin, Neal Spelce, news director at our CBS sister station KTBC, fed me details of the court's decision. Neal, who was the capital city's best news broadcaster, traded phone reports with me almost daily—each of us tagging the report "in Austin for KRLD News" and "in Dallas for KTBC News."

PRESS COVERAGE AND VENUE CHANGE

The judges held that precedent in trials of Dr. Sam Sheppard and Billie Sol Estes suggested that intense press coverage had prejudiced the Dallas jury pool, but the underlying rationale of the court went beyond the issue of press coverage. Appellate Judge W. T. McDonald wrote, "It is fair to assume that the citizenry of Dallas consciously felt Dallas was on trial and the Dallas image was uppermost in their minds to such an extent that Ruby could not be tried there fairly while the state, nation and world judged Dallas for the tragic November events."

Although our coverage was the factor that the court felt had mandated a venue change, underlying the issue of the defendant's rights was the question of the city's collective guilt complex, which McDonald suspected had damaged its impartiality beyond repair.

Presiding Judge W. A. Morrison wrote that Ruby's statements should have been excluded because they failed the legal test of spontaneity. Ruby had asked Secret Service chief Forrest Sorrels if his statements were to be for the press—too circumspect an attitude to be spontaneous. As for Pat Dean's testimony that Ruby had reported deciding to kill Oswald two nights before, Morrison told reporters that the admission "obviously constituted an oral confession of premeditation made while in police custody and therefore was not admissible."

When reporters met a happy Phil Burleson emerging from the jail after delivering the good news to his client, it appeared that Ruby had not
savored the triumph. "Jack wasn't crying or laughing," he told them. "We
just discussed seriously for about fifteen minutes the various possibilities
raised by the decision." The attorney said that excluding Pat Dean's testimony had destroyed the case for premeditation and therefore the case
for murder with malice, and he said that he planned to "work something
out with the state." Phil mentioned that he had made the argument for
murder without malice in his summations. He was too modest to mention that he'd been the only defense lawyer who'd argued that verdict to
the jury. Henry Wade responded that he would continue pressing the
charge of murder with malice. But none of that was going to make any
difference.

All the legal pullings and haulings, the high-profile attorneys, the
questions surrounding Jack Ruby's undeniable guilt—all that amounted
to nothing. Having seen his heroic act turn to disgrace, having listened
to his attorney compare him to the village idiot, having volunteered for
the polygraph exam that his mental state rendered inconclusive, the
once sparky Ruby had lost his panache. Jack was dying. He didn't know
that he would never live to be free, and neither did anyone else.

DOOMED TO PARKLAND

It was all slipping away for Jack, the tough guy who'd been proud of his
quick temper and the Chicago moniker it had earned him. His beloved
Sheba the dachshund was in the care of a former stripper, and despite
the sheriff's allowing some of Ruby's close friends to visit him, the
stubby little fellow was condemned to loneliness behind his own private bars. As his existence waned, he was about to embark upon the
loneliest of all journeys.

On the afternoon of December 9, 1966, Jack Ruby, sallow after three
years away from sunshine, was feeling so bad that Bill Decker called
the jail doctor. Jack was having trouble breathing, and Parkland doctors
admitted him just after five o'clock. He was losing strength, and the
symptoms suggested pneumonia. Nurses started intravenous drips,
and doctors ordered chest X-rays. It wasn't pneumonia.

As his miserable plight since that November Sunday had eaten away
his soul, a vast and aggressive malignancy had invaded his lungs.

Sandy Sanderson and I went to interview the jail doctor. The old veteran ran the big sound camera on a tripod while I asked the gaunt and timid physician to explain how Ruby's condition got past him. After grilling him for fifteen minutes, I could have summarized his answers as a shrug.

Jack Ruby, the deluded agent of justice, might have been running the Carousel Club if he hadn't dived into the limelight with a pistol. Now

Jack Ruby in happier times with stripper Tammi True. *Photograph courtesy The Sixth Floor Museum at Dealey Plaza. Photographer Jim MacCammon, Bob Huffaker Collection*

the old building was a gym for the Dallas Police Athletic Association. He lived his last month in Parkland.

I'd just finished doing the eleven o'clock radio news two mornings after New Year's Day of 1967, and Eddie and I were together in the newsroom when I answered our hotline. "Ruby's dead. Check it out," Bill Decker told me, then hung up, having given us the scoop. After I verified the news with Parkland, Eddie immediately fed a report to CBS, and I bulletined the wire services while he was talking. The long drama that had begun with the murder of a president had ended at last, with the fading of a chubby little man who had wept for JFK's widow, avenged his death, and unwittingly cheated history of answers.

Phil Burleson, who might have pled Ruby out of murder with malice and freed him with hardly more than time served, was in the Parkland room as Ruby slipped away that morning in the brand-new year.

They'd all ended up here: John Fitzgerald Kennedy, J. D. Tippit, Lee Harvey Oswald, and now Jack Leon Ruby. Eva Grant bent over the scrappy brother she'd stuck by, as Jack drifted out of his peculiar little life.

Bob Huffaker holds a microphone above interview with Judge Joe B. Brown and defense counsel Joe Tonahill. KRLD's Warren Fulks is behind Brown beside reporter Gordon Baxter. Gary DeLaune (lower left) takes notes beside defense attorney Joe Tonahill. *Photograph courtesy* Paris Match

LOOKING BACK

Dallas Love Field, June 15, 1964: Bob Huffaker (right) gets no response from 1964 GOP presidential candidate Senator Barry Goldwater as Texas GOP Senator John Tower and unsuccessful GOP congressional candidate George H. W. Bush watch. *Photograph courtesy AP/Wide World Photos*

10

Television, Radio, Ethics, and Duty

BOB HUFFAKER

KRLD deserves the highest praise for the manner in which its personnel moved without a moment of hesitation from what was to have been normal coverage of the arrival, presentation and departure of the President, into fascinating, elaborate, complete and deeply detailed coverage at the local level of what has to be easily the story of our modern lives.

> The Radio Television News Directors Association,
> presenting KRLD News its award for the
> nation's best on-the-spot reporting

Brooding over this entire story is the issue of journalistic objectivity among Dallas reporters accustomed to cooperating with police and firefighters. We knew that we were treading a fine line back then, but Eddie saw to it that we behaved with principle. We did not report selectively where police and fire personnel were concerned, although we knew these first-responders well and tried our best to help them.

My situation in the police basement, hung out on national television with my friend Sergeant Pat Dean, was historically unprecedented, and I tried to get as many facts as I could without compromising the officer's position. I was the rare reporter who had actually worn a badge and sidearm, and I knew enough of police procedure to understand that Pat couldn't finger a murderer by name until the decision had been made to charge the man with a crime.

Considering police procedure at such a moment was almost beside the point, since history's most public murder, even in those moments after the shooting, had left no doubt about Jack Ruby's identity and his having shot Lee Oswald. If I had known Ruby and distinguished his face in the wild pileup that ensued, I would have reported it myself without endangering the position of the police. But they observed established procedures for sound legal reasons, and wisely or not, I chose to work within them. Blurting out a killer's name is not what a good police officer would consider professional conduct.

I was in some respects like the so-called embedded reporters of today, now codified as "embeds." I had seen Pat in action as I rode with him on patrol, and having served as a part-time small-town cop, I knew a good officer when I saw one. Pat was as able and upright as they came. But, like today's embeds, I had to stick to objective or even adversarial standards of journalism—keeping in mind that it's hard to criticize people you've seen risking their lives to protect the rest of us.

But unlike reporters who rode hell-for-leather into Iraq with the troops, I had to be vigilant to report missteps of cops and firemen. The Dallas guys didn't make many, but when they did, we didn't cover them up. When Charlie Sansoni, an otherwise good detective well known for booking bets, finally was busted as a bookie, I was there with a camera and hot lights as Charlie covered his face.

We'd all joked with Sansoni and called him "the Dallas Mafia," but despite the petty nature of his crime, we reported it completely when it became news, even knowing that the disgrace had ruined his life. We knew not to cut the cops too much slack. But today's embedded war reporting lacks such adversarial freedom, with good reasons.

Covering soldiers differs from covering police. The embeds in the Middle East were in a position that limited their scope. Reporting selectively, they had to avoid interfering with the mission, endangering the troops, giving intelligence to the enemy, or encouraging the opposing forces. Such necessary constraints preclude reporting almost anything negative about troops in battle, but ethics bound us to reveal the flaws of civilian law enforcement. I had observed abusive cops firsthand in Central Texas, and I knew that police range from excellent and principled down to brutal and dishonest. In Dallas I never saw any bad cops in action, but I'm sure that there were some whose behavior I wouldn't have admired. Word on the street was that there were some bad cops, but we reporters were in daily contact with the good guys.

People become police for a variety of reasons, the noblest being to protect and serve, and the most deplorable being to bully and harass. Jack Ruby, who hurt unsteady drunks and offending strippers, was enchanted with the cops, but if he had been one, he'd have been the worst sort. Pat Dean, Jim Leavelle, Will Fritz, Jesse Curry, Jerry Hill, and the like were the best sort, committed to protecting the city and catching the bad guys. They didn't countenance mistreatment of suspects, and they didn't go looking for trouble. Police risk their lives riding herd on sometimes dangerous people, and they have enough trouble without looking for reasons to mess with folks.

I had admired John Guseman, the Bryan police chief, who had stood before his department and said, "OK, gentlemen, I want each of you to take out your wallet. Now open it up and read your commission card with me. It says that you are commissioned as a 'peace officer in the State of Texas.' The operative term here is 'peace'—not 'law enforcement.' Now get out there and preserve the peace of this community, and don't waste your time looking for some new law to enforce." That admonition was the mantra of most Dallas policemen. It was a big city, and they were too busy preserving the peace to put up with bullies on the force.

Officers pray for their slain comrade J. D. Tippit on Monday. Sgt. Jim Putnam is at right. *Photograph courtesy The Sixth Floor Museum at Dealey Plaza.* Dallas Times Herald *Collection*

As embedded journalists must take care not to interfere with military operations, we were careful not to get in the way of the cops and fire-fighters. They were doing a crucial and perilous job, and we respected them. In turn, they cooperated with us, allowing us much more freedom than is afforded reporters in these days of yellow crime-scene tape. In essence, we saw ourselves as two arms of the public trust. Their job was protecting citizens, and ours was informing them.

Like the first-responders, we faced danger in our duties. Our Steve Pieringer died when a gasoline storage tank exploded as he filmed fire enveloping it. I'd been with Steve at the middle of a similar fire in a cluster of such tanks, and when burning petroleum had flowed like lava under my mobile unit, I'd raced back to the station wagon and driven it out of the flames.

I routinely shot film from precarious angles, often inside burning buildings—young and foolish enough to show that I'd had the bravado to go into danger where the firemen went. Speed was crucial to us all. When the story was hot and the way clear, I drove those mobile units at ninety or more—once into a coastal hurricane that blasted the KRLD letters off the nose of that big Pontiac.

We reporters and the first-responders met each other in action constantly, and unlike the adversarial relationship that characterizes most of today's police-media relations, we tried to help each other out. But in one odd encounter I had continued to shoot footage while some misguided cop had tried to stop me from filming officers using only necessary force in subduing a fighting drunk. Then I had set up a projector in Jesse Curry's office and showed him the officer's behavior, after which he suspended the guy and issued a directive forbidding officers from interfering with any reporter just doing his job. That was before Jesse Curry met the national press.

In our newsroom, police and fire radio receivers hung above my desk, and like the rest of the KRLD News staff, I'd developed a tolerance to their constant chatter. We could tune out routine transmissions and glean important information from seven separate and simultaneous conversations. Two were frequencies of the sheriff's department, two others were those of the busy police, two were the more taciturn highway patrol, and one was the alarm system for the vast Dallas Fire Department. Listening to them, we knew how fast and urgently they moved. When the fire buzzers blared and the dispatcher said something like, "Six chief and seven engine, a house fire at 2814 Emmett Street," in less than thirty seconds we would hear the station's captain answer from the seat beside his engine driver, "Six chief and seven engine to 2814 Emmett." Behind the captain's voice we could hear the siren already building to a wail as the shiny truck gained speed. The whole engine company would be on their way in less than half a minute. They started, arrived, and extinguished fires in a hurry.

A joke in those days concerned a bragging Texan touring Italy and claiming that each of its sights was smaller than something in his native state. His guide showed him the erupting Vesuvius and said, "You don't have anything like that in Texas, do you?" to which he'd replied, "Well, no, but we got a fire department in Dallas that could put that sumbitch out inside of ten minutes."

I never met a fireman I didn't like—maybe because they're the sort to act upon the once-common boyhood dream of being a fireman. And after all, the brave and young at heart are the best kind of people.

I met a lot of such folks among the Dallas police, and their performance was as impressive as the firemen's. Their response time was amazingly quick. In the downtown district, they would be at the scene within a very few minutes, ready for action. I saw two squads arrive in a matter of seconds at the call of a construction site's night watchman who had seen intruders on the building's freshly poured second floor. Before determining that the suspects were concrete finishers come to retrieve their tools, the officers had scared hell out of the hapless crew. Still on the new second floor, the workmen had dropped their trowels and reached for heaven as cops below covered them with shotguns.

In those days of pencil and paper instead of digital electronics, the police dispatcher's room was a wonderland of efficiency. On either side of a long table sat six to ten people who took calls from those who phoned for police help. Down the table's midsection, a moving belt carried their messages to two radio dispatchers, whose microphones broadcast from the glassed-in adjoining room. The people who answered the phones wore headsets as they wrote the nature of each call and placed the completed form on the conveyer. In seconds, the paper was in the hands of a dispatcher, who sent a constant stream of calls to the patrol cars:

"Seventy-one, got a window peeper at 549 Westbrook."

And the reply from the car, "Seventy-one clear."

"Forty-nine, disturbance at the OK Bar, 734 Elm."

"Forty-nine clear."

Radio traffic was strictly business, but we heard occasional levity. I heard one Oak Cliff car receive a call about a loose monkey near the Marsalis Park Zoo, to which the officer replied, "You got a description on that monkey?"

It was easy to like our police and firemen, and as strange as it might sound in the twenty-first century, the mutual cooperation worked. Between us journalists and the guys who protected Dallas, we made the city both safer and better informed than it might have been without our mutual cooperation.

BEING DETACHED

Dallas wasn't alone in coziness between police and press. I'd seen and participated in similar cooperation in Central Texas, where its result was not always entirely salutary. I had faced conflict of interest by acting as both a reporter and a commissioned peace officer, even though I was playing cops and robbers principally for experience in police reporting. Some reporters were too easy on law enforcement people so as to ensure their access to them as sources of information. And some lawmen courted the press to the detriment of both public safety and public information. One of the most dangerous moves a law officer might make in those parts was to step between Texas Ranger Captain Clint Peoples and the nearest camera.

In Dallas, after Wes Wise had covered the Adlai Stevenson debacle, he entered upon a period of special cooperation with federal and local officers while they prepared to protect President Kennedy on his coming visit to the city. As Wes says, he was pushing journalistic ethics as he helped officers identify faces in the film he'd shot of the hate group that assaulted the ambassador, then as he helped the feds scan the Trade Mart crowd. But as I had tried to be simultaneously an ethical reporter and an honest cop, Wes, with his own sense of fairness and Eddie's guidance, had taken care to separate his professional and personal roles. When he'd been acting as journalist, he'd worn his press badge; while seated with his wife as a guest, he'd removed it and acted as a citizen on the lookout, helping the Secret Service protect the president—to no avail, as it turned out. Police protect, and journalists report. But it isn't always that simple.

Years earlier while I'd been covering a skydiving meet, one of the parachutists, a young woman, fell through thousands of feet as her chute roman-candled and refused to open, with its shroud lines entangled. Spectators screamed, and I watched in horror as she struggled in a fever to unsnarl the lines, plummeting toward inexorable death as she neared the ground. Somehow I found myself running toward her with my camera at my side, as if I might have somehow saved her. Disaster was happening before my very eyes, and I was reacting in a futile dash to stop it—knowing that I couldn't, but running at top speed nonetheless—and I wasn't taking pictures of the looming tragedy as a journalist is supposed to do.

I was still running, and she was a hundred feet from the ground when she cleared the lines. At the last second, the chute opened with a snap and swung her sideways once before she touched down and rolled to a stop. My protective instincts, however powerless at the moment, had taken over as she fell, and my journalist's instincts had failed me.

The girl was safe, the drama was over, and I had no pictures of it. But I had learned about the sort of ethical paradox we faced in Dallas. Do you merely record tragedy, or do you also try to avert it? Wes and I, like Eddie and others in the Dallas press, tried to strike a balance between our professional duty to report news and our human duty to help protect our fellow mortals. When we were forced to choose either pragmatic human considerations or rigid reportorial detachment, our humanity often won the day. And for more than half my life, I have known that Jack Ruby couldn't have shot Lee Oswald if we of the fourth estate hadn't been taking our own shots that Sunday morning.

THE WORLD COMES TO TELEVISION

When we obliterated Japanese cities and ended the Second World War, the world was on the radio. Our imaginations drew the pictures while entertainment and news came to us as sound—the language, noise and music that connected us to the world, linked us to our fellow man, warned us, and calmed our fears.

Eight years old, I stood in the yard and listened to President Truman tell us about the bomb. During those long days of sacrifice, fear and

uncertainty, amplitude-modulated—AM—radio had held our world together, often through interfering transatlantic static, telling us of death
and hope, tragedy and victory—letting us hear the bombs exploding,
warning families like mine near Texas coastal refineries when danger
might approach from the night air.

Kids like Bill Mercer and Jim Underwood were over there fighting for
the rest of us. Kids like Wes Wise were getting ready to wear the uniform in the Korean War, and kids like George Phenix, Eddie Barker
and I were listening to the radio and learning about the atomic bomb
that had killed populations to save us.

During that great war, reporters like Edward R. Murrow and the young
Walter Cronkite gripped microphones and handsets to tell America of
bombs falling on London, of children dying young, of stubborn Brits who
put out fires and drank tea in the rubble, of our advancing troops, and of
boys who wouldn't be coming back. Wooden round-topped radios kept
us in touch with a world fallen into conflict, and all of us—Cronkite,
Rather, Schieffer, Barker, Wise, Mercer, Phenix and I—grew up when
the world was on the radio, and the only living pictures of it were newsreels after the fact before the movie cartoons.

After the war, we saw crowds in front of furniture and appliance stores,
pressing the plate glass to see the new thing called a television, which
broadcast a movie film or a live picture—just as radios, by then mostly
cased in plastic instead of wood, picked up sound waves from the air.

When we youngsters started talking on the radio, TV was developing as a news medium, and most of television's newsmen had learned
broadcast journalism in radio. As we put pictures with sound, we
learned to use television's obvious capabilities beyond those of radio.
Broadcast journalism has evolved along with technology of sound and
video recording: from Edison's cylinder through the 78 rpm, 45 rpm,
then $33\frac{1}{3}$ rpm disk, through wire recorders, reel-to-reel tapes, high-fi,
stereo, cartridges and cassettes, toward today's digital reproduction of
picture and sound.

Walter Cronkite had broadcast the first news of the tragic three shots
while viewers saw only a lettered bulletin slide on the screen. He had
been unable to address a CBS camera because none was warmed up.
In 1963 we still relied upon vacuum tubes as well as the newly developed transistor, and our sound cameras used film with an optical sound
track alongside the reel of framed pictures. Hold the developed film to

light, and you would see the squiggly white line that reproduced sound as it passed through a projector.

There were only two satellites: Telstar bounced microwaves to Europe, and Relay had just begun reflecting them to Asia. JFK had taped a greeting to Asia for Relay's official inauguration, which was to fall upon the day of his death. Microwave relay was the newest way to send a broadcast signal, but television and radio news methods were barely beyond the Stone Age compared to today's era of cybernetics and digital electronics. And now, although frequency-modulated radio—FM, barely noticed in the sixties—sends a static-free signal beyond quality of AM radio, television remains the prime news medium that it became on November 22, 1963.

At Eddie's sad news from the Trade Mart and Walter Cronkite's choked words as he removed his glasses at the network desk, at the riderless horse trotting behind the murdered president's caisson, the mourning nation drew together around a glowing black-and-white picture tube. For the first time, live television was bonding them as witnesses to their own living history—uniting them with shared news of tragedy, uncertainty and hope.

Now the world was on the television, where it remains to this day, in color—dividing as much as uniting those who watch the screen.

11
Broadcast News, Fifty Years After

We begin to think less in terms of responsibility and integrity, which get you in trouble . . . and more in terms of power and money. . . . Suck-up coverage is in.

Dan Rather

THE BOTTOM OF THE SEA CHANGE—GEORGE PHENIX

The events of 1963 marked a sea change in the way people wanted to get their news. Prior to the assassination, most Americans trusted their hometown newspaper more than their local television station. It wasn't official until it was in the printed headlines. Most major cities even had two newspapers—a morning and an afternoon paper.

When the president was murdered, old newsreels show people gathering outside their local newspapers waiting either for the special edition or for the afternoon paper. But around-the-clock coverage quickly shifted focus to television. We wanted more information, and we wanted it faster. Somehow it helped us to understand what had happened to our nation.

Then when Ruby shot Oswald on national TV, the shift from newspapers to TV was sealed. And television rose to meet the new responsibility. The nation and the world were united in grief and wonder as the cameras helped us share the tragedy. People stayed in their living rooms with their families and the television set.

Television news got better. Electronic giants roamed the land—Walter Cronkite, David Brinkley, and Chet Huntley, to name three. Technology improved to allow live coverage of fast-breaking events like the riots in

Huffaker, Wise, Mercer, Phenix (L to R).

Chicago during the Democratic National Convention and the Watergate hearings. Without question, television helped bring about the end of the Vietnam War. Political spinmeisters began to time their candidate's sound bites to take advantage of the news cycle for maximum exposure.

People actually hurried home from work so they could watch the evening news. And afternoon newspapers began to close shop throughout the nation. TV news stayed in power for several decades. It was the glory days for young journalists who looked good and talked good. Salaries skyrocketed.

But it was too good to last. Cable ruined television news, in my opinion. TV news has sunk to new lows. Consider this: you are watching a cable television news show when suddenly a pop-up and loud music announce a "News Alert." Am I the only one who thinks that is redundant?

If the anchor person is on the air giving you the news, why must they interrupt themselves to tell you about even more news via the asinine *News Alert!*

And why must Fox News tell you over and over again that their news is "Fair and Balanced" unless they are trying to sell the concept they only tentatively believe. Is there even one viewer who does not know that Fox is the most conservative of the cable news systems? The "Fair and Balanced" patina has worn a little thin.

In 1963, if our news wasn't fair and balanced, Eddie Barker would fire us. That's how we defined fair and balanced.

At this point, however, I must adjust my self-inflicted halo. Then and now, television shares a weakness—the problem of not enough time to explain the story fully, which allows media-savvy elected officials to "stay on message" rather than answer the damn question.

Another problem that hasn't gone away with the passage of time: inexperienced reporters are asked to conduct interviews on subjects way over their heads. Sometime in 1964, I was assigned to interview Dr. Edward Teller, the scientist who helped invent the H-bomb, a bona fide genius. When I whined that I didn't know anything about the man or his work, one of my cohorts at the station handed me a *Time* magazine which had a story about Dr. Teller, with this advice: "Read this next time you go the bathroom."

Recently I was interviewed by a television reporter who was totally unprepared. I had gone to the trouble to e-mail background information about the interview, but the reporter had not read any of it. With the camera running, she tried to skim the material and form intelligent questions at the same time. Finally I began to interrupt her with prompts: "Be sure you ask me about thus and so." I was embarrassed for her.

What's the upshot of this mini-gripe session? I think TV news has lost the ethical and moral high ground and is in danger of losing audience, too.

Americans have become turned off by the news. There's a reason that journalists rank at the bottom of popularity polls below even trial lawyers. We have become exposed as obnoxious in our pursuit of the story. The audience doesn't believe its government or its news outlets. Conspiracy theories abound about almost everything.

So where do people go for their news? A growing number go to the Internet, where they can find website after website that agrees with their perception of major events. Witness the many websites about the Kennedy assassination. Pick your favorite conspiracy theory—the Cubans, the government, the Mafia—and you can find somebody on the Net with a site that adds torque to your particular warp.

For me, the question is: has TV news helped make America smarter? Or dumber? I vote for the latter. I think the pandering to the lowest common denominator has given rise to the so-called survivor shows and voyeur programs that feature banal activities of cheap celebrities. Unfortunately, the news shows are not far behind.

In 1963, not only did I ride with the police on drug raids, sometimes I would drink beer with the cops after we all got off work. We were cozy—probably too cozy. I thought I could maintain objectivity and even got chewed out by the cops after one particular drug bust story. Maybe I could. But, with hindsight, I believe the perception of fairness suffered.

That may be one of the reasons that Dallas Police Chief Curry made the reluctant and fateful decision to let the press view the transfer of Oswald from the city to the county jail—a decision that cost Oswald his life.

After the incriminations settled, I'm sure both journalism schools and police schools around the nation used the Dallas fiasco as a how-not-to laboratory for police/press relations. Never again would a police department lean over so far to accommodate the press. The U.S. military learned the same lesson during Vietnam, where they allowed reporters almost unlimited access to troops in the field. But no more.

Interestingly, for years political reporters would accept free rides on candidates' planes as they flew across the election fields. Fortunately, that practice has evolved to a system whereby reporters still fly on campaign airplanes, but they pay a pro rata share for the cost of a ticket.

RADIO TELEVISION NEWS: THEN AND NOW— WES WISE

Although journalism today—especially radio-television journalism—benefits greatly from the technological advances of the last forty or so years, the overall quality of reporting was superior at the time of President Kennedy's assassination.

The "street reporter" of those times enjoyed much better relations with law enforcement, was better informed on a variety of subjects, and was more savvy overall. As a result there were more genuine "scoops" in a more competitive environment.

The immediacy of television satellite transmission is unequalled in terms of up-to-the-minute information. However, the final on-the-air product frequently suffers from the prevalence of the news story "package." The end product often intersperses tiny interview sound bites with video pictures of the scene, resulting in a hodgepodge of confusing sequences with quotes taken completely out of context from the reporter's original question. Worse, the quotes are often placed in an entirely different context, which is often unfair to the person being interviewed.

The role of the producer has become paramount, while the role of the journalist has become minor. Frequently the interviewer-journalist is not even pictured, increasing the likelihood of the quote's being out of context.

In 1963 the spirit of friendly but determined competition between television-radio news gatherers was greater than it is today. In current TV for instance, identical video will show up on competing stations and networks. This repetition is especially noticeable in sports coverage where the same tape of the same run or pass from the same angle is patently obvious, but it is as often seen in hard news coverage. In the old days of 16 mm film, the television station prided itself on better shots at better angles and getting the film back to the newsroom quicker in order to best the competition. Of course the viewer was the principal beneficiary of such intense competition.

In many cases today the lines have been blurred between news and commercialism. Over and above the admitted "infomercial," many news commentators today gently segue from news story to commercial and back again, frequently confusing the listener or viewer. The unbelievable proliferation of "all news" stations and networks further complicates the confusion. Should a radio or television station or network that promotes itself incessantly as "twenty-four-hour news" deluge the airways with infomercial programs that drone on and on? Would Edward R. Murrow or Walter Cronkite ever consider doing a commercial on a news broadcast?

The lines have become even more blurred between journalism and political commentary. This situation has become almost laughable in recent times, with one all-news cable network billing itself as having more "balanced" news compared to those other guys. Of course, the accusations that the mainstream press is covertly liberal have become

legion even as the conservative talk show hosts have come to dominate the radio airways.

In the early 1960s KRLD radio launched *Comment,* the first talk show
in Dallas. Every person who went on the air on this program was an established journalist working for both the television station and the radio
station. The program originated from the newsroom, and that fact was
clearly stated. Listeners were clearly informed that these were journalists. Although opinions were encouraged from listeners by telephone, the
hosts carefully avoided personal opinions, leaving that prerogative to
Comment listeners. This is balanced journalism by journalists.

In spite of this criticism the fact remains that today's saturation television and radio coverage of outstanding news events is unequalled, and it
all began with November 22, 1963. Such coverage reached another
zenith with the terrorist attacks of 9/11.

In the future, what major events will radio and television news be
ready to cover?

IMAGINE—BILL MERCER

Take today's radio and television technology back to November 22, 1963,
and imagine how news professionals would have handled the event and
how their coverage would have appeared to viewers and listeners.

With satellite availability, the entire event starting with President
Kennedy's landing at Love Field would have been—in the words of the
old cliché—"live and in color." Satellite trucks of every television channel would have been lined up end to end at the airport broadcasting
live as the dignitaries arrived. The place would have been crawling with
reporters and cameras in far greater numbers than those that greeted
JFK and his party.

Just like Macy's big parade, the procession into downtown Dallas
would have passed other satellite trucks with fixed and hand-held video
cameras and reporters describing the color and the enormous crowd wel-
coming the president. Had there been helicopters then equipped with
the satellite cameras we have today, there would have been intriguing
views of the great parade. However, today the airspace would be closed;
then we were still a very open nation.

The most troublesome part of this picture is the probability that the
actual assassination of the president might have been broadcast live. A

horrifying sight might have greeted viewers—the gruesome scene of the final shot blasting away part of the president's head, comparable only to the live telecast of the Twin Towers collapsing on 9/11.

The somber and emotionally draining picture at Parkland, captured in stark black and white film, would have been a circus of camera operators and reporters scrambling and speculating, using today's technology. Would the gravity and dignity of the coverage have been lost?

The influx of all varieties of reporters in 1963 created pandemonium on the third floor of the police station where Lee Harvey Oswald, his family and others were paraded throughout the night of the assassination. If that reporting mob had possessed today's easy ability to broadcast live on both television and radio, the scene would have been awesome—although today's reporters would have no such open access precisely because of what happened in Dallas police headquarters in 1963. Transpose the scene of the O. J. Simpson trial and today's other hyped celebrity legal doings to our post-assassination reporting, and one can imagine something on the order of Super Bowl mayhem.

In 1963 the police and city officials were attempting to be as accommodating as possible so that the press could transmit the truth of the developing story to the public. Today there would be no press mob on the third floor, no public display of the assassin being moved, and certainly no after-midnight press conference with the accused. Maybe or maybe not, the full and true story might have been told by high-tech reporting had it been available back then. What we covered in 1963 with black-and-white film would, and does, seem primitive.

With the expanded cable news outlets of today and their various political leanings, conspiracy theories would have proliferated faster. Ratings-driven reporters would have hammered all related persons and peripheral stories. Pundits would have commented. Experts would have speculated.

Then there is the horrendous spectacle of "talk radio." The majority of these ego-driven programs cater to the right-wing or conservative audience. If they had existed in 1963, conspiracy theories would have run amok. Recall the carefully scripted stories of events in the President Clinton era that these talk shows accepted as gospel. Now expand such misinformation to include theories blaming LBJ, Fidel Castro, the mob, the FBI, the CIA, a left-wing plot to blame conservatives, and of course Richard Nixon, who was in Dallas that day. Radio talk shows like today's would have soon created at least as much confusion about the facts as Oliver Stone's *JFK* spawned years later.

Had today's attention to rights of the accused been practiced in 1963, Oswald might not have been executed in the basement of the police station but instead gone to trial, where the truth—the reasons and motives of the assassination—might have been revealed. But technology alone does not bring lawbreakers to justice, and today's extensive press coverage of trials doesn't necessarily provide a clear view of the truth.

In light of the tragedy in November of 1963, such an open parade of the president, vice president and a state's governor will never again be staged. Today the nation's two top elected officials are seen together only in carefully secured locations with an equally carefully selected audience. And the nation's two top officials are never together at promotional speeches or fund-raising events.

The country changed on November 22, 1963—and not for the better.

THE HERD INSTINCT—BOB HUFFAKER

I sat behind the radio news console across the table from Robert Pierpoint, the CBS White House correspondent. He leaned into the mike and said, "Testing, one two three" as I set his level on my VU meter. The shapeless little fellow had asked me to record the report, which was to air on one of those early anniversaries of November 22. Maybe it was the first anniversary, in 1964; I don't recall. My memories of that tragedy wash together like watercolors.

I'd sent a car to fetch the CBS man when his plane landed at Love Field, and he'd approached me at the news desk, where I was broadcasting on the hour and assembling my long ten o'clock nightly newscast. Pierpoint wanted to tape his special Dallas anniversary report and relay it to New York. We local guys were always ready to oblige.

I rolled the tape and gave him the nod. "They say that Dallas is not a city of hate," he began. "And yet, on the streets of Dallas, one gets the impression—" he continued. Then to my amazement he characterized Dallas as a center of political extremism and distrust, then went on to imply that some vaguely defined sense of unease and hatred still lurked in the city where he'd landed not a half-hour earlier.

He ended the report, "This is Robert Pierpoint, CBS News, in Dallas." To be sure, he had actually done the feed from Dallas. Its overriding impression was that he had taken time to gauge the mood of the city, but I marveled that he'd managed to accomplish his analysis in a ten-minute ride from the airport.

Pierpoint was parroting the media line—Dallas was a city of hate after all—and apparently one could draw that conclusion by landing at Love Field and riding to our newsroom. His broadcast wouldn't air for several days, when he would have since left Dallas. If this was what reporters did, I didn't want to be a reporter. I handed the pale little man the tape reel, told him he could take a cab to his hotel, and walked back into the teletype room.

The CBS correspondent Harry Reasoner had used my desk and left me a fifth of Old Forester, almost full, in its lower right drawer. Like Walter Cronkite, Reasoner was a seasoned wartime reporter with a straight approach to the facts, and I never heard such an abomination from him, but Pierpoint was obviously misleading his audience by reporting things he had not investigated.

The CBS icon Eric Sevareid spent time in our newsroom, too. On a Sunday, his producer had asked me where she and Mr. Sevareid might have lunch. I'd referred them to the scruffy Gaston Cafeteria, across from Baylor Hospital, where Dean Angel and I stoked ourselves with cheap meals. They'd driven past it and decided at a single glance that it wasn't the place for them. Even though Sevareid was dean of CBS commentators, he depended on his producer for lunch. And for his facts, he depended largely upon his research staff.

Not long after I broadcast the Oswald shooting, Sevareid's office had called me to discuss how such a debacle might have been allowed to happen. His staff talked to me several times that day, during which I explained Ruby's entry through tight security just as I would explain it now after four decades. Ruby's breaching police security to shoot the handcuffed prisoner was a rare chance, I told them, exacerbated by the mob of reporters. But when I saw Eric Sevareid's commentary on the CBS Evening News that day, he mentioned nothing of what I'd said. Instead, he grouped the police and sheriff's department into "Dallas Law Enforcement," which was at fault for failing to protect Oswald. Thanks to his research staff, even Sevareid, a lion among commentators, was sticking to the expected line: blame Dallas, the city that killed the president.

Today's media tends toward following the bell cow as well, and the herd instinct is one of its greatest weaknesses, more pronounced today than it was four decades ago. As a result, an officeholder's misadventures trump reporting about his public service; anyone unopposed to gun ownership is assumed to be a trigger-happy madman; political labeling replaces news about issues: "liberals" are all wimpy dreamers, and "conservatives" are all greedy and heartless. Meanwhile, television news feeds viewers a steady diet of police chases, celebrity rapes and murders, dog bites, domestic strife, and the latest sexy developments on some infernal "reality" show. Reporting about public affairs is short on independent research and long on shallow sound bites from opposing politicians. News is delivered in present participles and often covered like traffic, from a helicopter. Such bland and trivial reporting is less risky for broadcast journalists, cheaper to produce, inoffensive to partisans, and ultimately unenlightening to citizens who seldom learn the import of events that affect their nation and their world.

In these days when cynicism and partisanship are making inroads among the media, calling up the notion that "Ye shall know the truth, and the truth shall make thee free" has come to sound naïve and sentimental. Nonetheless, we four old newsmen have devoted our lives to that ideal, and we still believe it. When the meaning of words such as *fair* and *balanced* is lost amid hype that masks slanting news for political ends, the principles of journalistic objectivity are in danger. And when journalists, whose mantra has been objective reporting of facts, acquiesce in favoring a particular political ideology, the nation's freedom and the world's pursuit of peace are in danger.

None of us has been a political commentator nor wished to be one, and we have always believed in the ideal of freedom of speech and press, as well as openness in government, with the attendant freedom of press access to public officials, meetings, and records. With ever more sophisticated partisan ploys to deny such access, freedom of the press is under siege.

Journalists have been to blame for many of the problems they now face daily. In 1963 we saw their incivility in Dallas police headquarters, some of them no more dignified or principled than paparazzi, and we saw their blindness to facts that contradicted the herd's reporting line. As Dallasites we regretted the oversimple reporting that encouraged the world to blame the entire city for acts of a left-wing assassin, a small cadre of right-wing extremists, and a morning newspaper with ultraconservative tunnel vision. As reporters we tried to show all sides of issues—not merely the two polar opposites, as today's trend seems to demand.

Given the ills of the media's herd instinct, reporting of politics and government has retreated to pacifying the adversarial extremes, with antipodal opinions pitted against each other and moderate views often left unnoticed and unreported somewhere in the middle. Corporate money and political power have gained considerable leverage upon news reporting, and moderation doesn't sell to the public nearly as well as bellicose superpatriotism on the right, prudish political correctness on the left, and *ad hominem* argument from both sides. Covering only the clash between political extremes, with shouting pundits reciting opposing ideologies, is no virtue among journalists—and reporting with investigative diligence the many sides of issues that concern mankind is no vice.

Except for disasters, wars, or rumors of war, U.S. viewers seldom see news from other countries, and the Bush II administration exploited that national ignorance to launch its disastrous Iraq invasion—fooling credulous reporters and attacking inquisitive ones. It tried to hide questionable motives and unquestionable ineptitude by the age-old ploy of blaming the press for reporting the bad news of its misadventures, equating truthful reporting with "emboldening the enemy" and "not supporting the troops."

While journalists were dying along with the troops, the administration undermined public confidence in the press by planting a ringer among White House reporters and bribing pundits to recite propaganda. CBS took down the reporter's reporter Dan Rather after bloggers assailed some documents in his accurate story about the president's brief and undistinguished Texas Air National Guard service.

In contrast, President Barack Obama's administration has treated the media with cautious civility—except for the implacable right-wing Fox channel. Legitimate reporters, meanwhile, confront the administration about issues like domestic surveillance and drone strikes against terrorists—particularly those who might be U.S. citizens. Unlike reporters who abandoned due diligence in the tragic stampede to Iraq, good ones still cover dangerous Mideast developments, risking their lives to publish truth whether or not it pleases the powerful.

As broadcast and print journalism evolves along with expanded roles of blogging, web searching, and other Internet capabilities, we face the question of which information sources to believe in the collision of technology and politics. Satirical news presentations by *The Daily Show with Jon Stewart* and *The Colbert Report* have become more astute than much of the so-called mainstream media in asking inconvenient questions of those in power. Meanwhile, too much of the media neglects real news while flooding us with detailed hypercoverage of young blond women who are missing or misbehaving. As long as shallow sensationalism sells today's news and supplants the reporting of complex issues, the journalistic community is in retreat from its function as an arm of a civil and humane society.

And so in memory I stand with a microphone among the cheering crowd in the canyons of downtown Dallas. It is forever 1963, and the cold and gray autumn morning has given way to balmy and sun-drenched noon on a perfect day. The popular young president and his elegant wife are smiling and greeting the crowds that line the bunting-festooned streets, as confetti and ticker tape flow from skyscraper windows above.

I have dreamed of him. He towers over me in the dream like a bronze statue, walking forward at a hurried pace, with a barely perceptible limp from the back trouble that nags us both. We are walking together, and I am having difficulty keeping up with him as he moves on looking straight ahead. He looks down at me, bending slightly, an animated monument at my side. He is in a hurry as I struggle to keep up. I listen but cannot hear what he is saying.

And then I am back at Main and Akard. Forever they pass, his bronze skin like the statue. Forever they are young and beautiful. Forever they smile and wave. Forever they are whisked by me in a glittering limousine, and the crowd surges out to meet them, to follow the last press busses away toward Dealey Plaza. Forever the crowd closes behind them as they fade from sight in a swirl of confetti. Forever the sun is straight overhead, and red, white and blue bunting glows in the autumn sunshine.

. . . Now the trumpet summons us again—not as a call to bear arms, though arms we need—not as a call to battle, though embattled we are—but a call to bear the burden of a long twilight struggle, year in and year out, 'rejoicing in hope, patient in tribulation'—a struggle against the common enemies of man: tyranny, poverty, disease and war itself.

Can we forge against these enemies a grand and global alliance, North and South, East and West, that can assure a more fruitful life for all mankind? Will you join in that historic effort?

In the long history of the world, only a few generations have been granted the role of defending freedom in its hour of maximum danger. I do not shrink from this responsibility—I welcome it. I do not believe that any of us would exchange places with any other people or any other generation. The energy, the faith, the devotion which we bring to this endeavor will light our country and all who serve it—and the glow from that fire can truly light the world.

And so, my fellow Americans: ask not what your country can do for you—ask what you can do for your country.

My fellow citizens of the world: ask not what America will do for you, but what together we can do for the freedom of man.

—President John Fitzgerald Kennedy
From the Inaugural Address, January 20, 1961

INDEX

Note: Italic page numbers refer to photographs.